THiNK

STUDENT'S BOOK 2

B1

Herbert Puchta, Jeff Stranks & Peter Lewis-Jones

CAMBRIDGE
UNIVERSITY PRESS

CONTENTS

PRONUNCIATION	THINK	SKILLS	
Intonation and sentence stress	**Values:** Human qualities **Self-esteem:** Personal qualities	Reading	Online survey responses: Who do you admire most? TV programme preview: Britain's Smartest Kids Photostory: The new café
		Writing	A short passage about someone you admire
		Listening	Playing a guessing game
Word stress	**Values:** Learning for life **Train to Think:** Learning about texts	Reading	Article: An education like no other Article: Learning is brain change Culture: A day in the life of …
		Writing	An email describing your school routine
		Listening	Conversation about a book
Words ending in /ə/	**Values:** Spending wisely **Self-esteem:** The film of my life	Reading	Article: Big movies on a small budget TV listings: different types of programmes Photostory: Extras
		Writing	A paragraph about your TV habits
		Listening	Interview with a teenage filmmaker
The short /ʌ/ vowel sound	**Values:** Responsible online behaviour **Train to Think:** Logical sequencing	Reading	Article: Think before you act online Short texts: Different types of messages Culture: Communication through history
		Writing	A web page giving advice
		Listening	Conversation about installing a computer game
Been: strong /biːn/ and weak /bɪn/	**Values:** Following your dreams **Self-esteem:** Music and me	Reading	Online forum: Singer songwriter: Any advice? Article: John Otway – Rock's greatest failure Photostory: Pop in the park
		Writing	The story of your favourite band
		Listening	Interviews about music
/f/, /v/ and /b/ consonant sounds	**Values:** Caring for the world **Train to Think:** Different perspectives	Reading	Article: Hot topic: The environment Leaflet: Small changes, BIG consequences Culture: Stop! Before it's too late
		Writing	An article for the school magazine
		Listening	Interviews about a town project

WELCOME

A GETTING TO KNOW YOU
Introducing yourself

1 Read the letter quickly. Write the names under the photos.

Hi Paulo,

My name's Nicola and I'd like to be your pen pal. I got your name from my teacher, Miss Edwards. She lived in Brazil for three years, and she's a good friend of your mother's.

So what would you like to know about me? I'm 15 years old. I live in a small house in Manchester with my mum and my two little brothers. They're OK, but they can be annoying sometimes. I go to Bluecoat High School. I quite like school, but my teachers always give us too much homework. I usually do it when I get home from school, but I'm not doing that today – that's because I'm writing to you!

I like listening to music and playing games on the computer. I also like playing the guitar. I play in a band with some of my friends. I like sport, too. I play volleyball and tennis. I'm in the school tennis team. We usually play matches on Saturday mornings. That's a bit of a problem because I don't really like getting up early at the weekend.

But what about you? I hope you'll want to write to me. There are lots of questions I want to ask you. Things like: what's life like in Brazil? Do you like your school? What's it like? What's the weather like in Rio? Have you got a big family? All that sort of stuff, to help me get to know you. Miss Edwards says you like surfing, but that's all I know about you.

So please write. I'd love to have a Brazilian friend.

Best

Nicola

2 Read the letter and complete the form about Nicola.

Name *Nicola*   Hometown _____
Age _____ Family   _____
Likes _____
Dislikes _____

Asking questions

3 Match the questions with the answers to make mini-dialogues.

1 What do you do? ☐
2 What are you doing? ☐
3 What do you like doing? ☐
4 Do you like studying English? ☐
5 Where are you from? ☐
6 Are you 14? ☐

a I'm watching TV.
b Yes, it's great.
c I'm from Italy.
d I'm a student.
e No, I'm 13.
f I love playing tennis.

4 [SPEAKING] Work in pairs. Ask and answer the questions in Exercise 3. Give answers that are true for you.

5 Choose the next line for each of the mini-dialogues in Exercise 3.

1 What's your teacher's name?
2 Do you live in Rome?
3 What school do you go to?
4 When is your birthday?
5 Would you like to go out and do something with me?
6 Me too. Do you want to come over and play the new Angry Birds game?

6 [SPEAKING] Work in pairs. Think of one more line for each dialogue. Then practise your dialogues.

What do you do?   I'm a student.

What school do you go to?

St Mark's High School in York.

Miami

Rio

London

Oslo

Istanbul

The weather

1 What kind of weather do you love, like or hate? Draw a 😄, 🙂 or a 🙁 next to each one.

- ☐ sunny ◯
- ☐ wet ◯
- ☐ cloudy ◯
- ☐ warm ◯
- ☐ cold ◯
- ☐ windy ◯
- ☐ humid ◯
- ☐ rainy ◯
- ☐ dry ◯
- ☐ freezing ◯
- ☐ hot ◯
- ☐ foggy ◯

2 **SPEAKING** Work in pairs. Tell your partner.

I love rainy weather.

3 🔊 1.02 Listen to the weather forecast for the UK. Tick (✓) the weather words in Exercise 1 that you hear.

4 🔊 1.02 Listen again. What is the weather going to be like in Manchester, Birmingham and London?

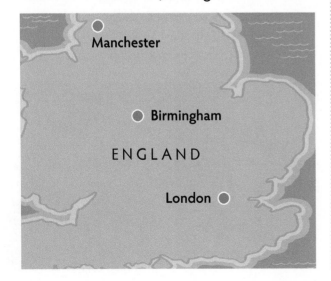

◯ Manchester

◉ Birmingham

ENGLAND

London ◉

5 **SPEAKING** Work in pairs. Look at the pictures. Ask and answer questions.

What's the weather like in Miami?

It's windy and very wet.

Families

1 Look at the family words. Complete the pairs.

1 mother and _____
2 brother and _____
3 aunt and _____
4 grandma and _____
5 husband and _____
6 cousin and _____

2 🔊 1.03 Listen to Nicola talking to Paulo on Skype. How are these people related to Nicola?

1 Colin _____
2 Luke _____
3 Sharon _____
4 Becky _____
5 Jodie _____
6 Mike _____
7 Jamie _____
8 Kai _____
9 Shay _____
10 Joe _____

3 **SPEAKING** Work in pairs. Ask each other about your families.

Have you got any cousins?

What's your uncle's name?

5

B EXPERIENCES
Meeting people

1 Put the parts of dialogue in order. Write 1–10 in the boxes.

	A	Really! Where? When?
	A	What book was it?
	A	Did he give you one?
1	A	Have you ever met a famous person?
	A	Did you say anything to him?
	B	It was my English course book, believe it or not. I had it with me to help me with my English.
	B	Yes, he was really nice. I didn't have any paper with me, so he signed a book that I was carrying.
	B	It was last summer. We were on holiday in LA. We were walking out of a restaurant when he walked in.
	B	Yes, I did. I asked him for an autograph.
	B	Yes, I have. Bradley Cooper.

2 🔊 1.04 Listen and check.

3 SPEAKING Work with a partner. Practise the conversation. Change names, places and other details.

4 Underline examples of the following tenses in Exercise 1.

1 A past simple positive statement.
2 A past simple negative statement.
3 A past simple question.
4 A past simple short answer.
5 A past continuous statement.
6 A present perfect question with *ever*.
7 A present perfect short answer.

Irregular past participles

1 Write the past participles of these irregular verbs.

1	think	_____	7	eat	_____
2	drink	_____	8	make	_____
3	wear	_____	9	run	_____
4	see	_____	10	win	_____
5	lose	_____	11	read	_____
6	hear	_____	12	ride	_____

2 Complete the questions with eight of the past participles in Exercise 1.

1 Who's the most famous person you've ever _seen_ ?
2 What's the strangest food you've ever _____ ?
3 What's the best book you've ever _____ ?
4 What's the funniest joke you've ever _____ ?
5 What's the most expensive thing you've ever _____ and never found again?
6 What's the best prize you've ever _____ ?
7 What are the most embarrassing clothes you've ever _____ ?
8 What's the longest phone call you've ever _____ ?

3 Answer the questions in Exercise 2 with your own information. Give details.

The most famous person I've ever seen is Lionel Messi.

4 Work in groups of eight. Each person takes one of the questions from Exercise 2 and thinks of two more questions to ask.

Who's the most famous person you've ever seen?
Where did you see him/her?
Did you say anything to him/her?

5 SPEAKING Ask the other students in your group your questions.

6 SPEAKING Report back to the group.

The most famous person Carla has seen is Lionel Messi. She saw him outside a shop in Barcelona. She didn't say anything to him.

Losing things

1 Read the story and find the answer to the question.

What was in the wrong container?

People often complain about airline companies losing their suitcases when they fly. It's never happened to me, but something a lot worse happened to my family recently.

About ten years ago my mum got a job teaching at a university in Indonesia. At first she only went for six months, but she really liked it and agreed to stay longer, so we all went to live with her. We had a great time, but last year my parents decided that they wanted to return to the UK. Because we'd been there so long we had loads of things we wanted to take back with us – all the furniture from our house in fact.

So mum and dad went to a shipping company and arranged to take everything back in one of those big containers that you see on ships. The company packed everything into it: the armchair and sofas, the TV, wardrobes, desks, even all the carpets and curtains. Our whole house was inside that big green metal box.

We flew back to the UK and waited for the container to arrive. About ten weeks later we were having breakfast one morning when a big lorry arrived outside our house. On the back was a big green metal box. We were so excited. The men opened the container and started to take out our things. But they weren't our things. The container was full of motorbikes. It was the wrong one. My parents were so annoyed. But the story has a happy ending. The men took the container and motorbikes away, and about two months ago our things finally arrived.

2 Read the story again and answer the questions. Use the word in brackets in your answer.

1 When did Liam's mum start her job in Indonesia? (ago)

2 When did the family move to Indonesia? (later)

3 How long did they stay there? (about)

4 When did they decide to move back to the UK? (last)

5 How long after they were back in the UK did the first container arrive? (about)

6 When did the correct container finally arrive? (ago)

3 WRITING Write a short story about something you lost. Use these questions to help you.

- When did it happen?
- What was it?
- Where did you lose it?
- What did you do?
- How did you feel?
- Did you find it? If so, when and where?

Furniture

1 Tick (✓) the items mentioned in the story.

2 SPEAKING Name the other items. Which of these do you think Liam's parents probably didn't put into the container?

They probably didn't put the toilet into the container.

3 Discuss in small groups.

Your family is moving to the other side of the world. They are packing the house things into a container, but there is only room for five items. What five items of furniture from your house are you going to choose?

C EATING AND DRINKING
Buying and talking about food

1 🔊 1.05 **Listen and complete each space with one word.**

ASSISTANT	Morning, can I help you?
CUSTOMER	Yes, please. Um, I want ¹_____ onions.
ASSISTANT	OK, how many?
CUSTOMER	Two kilos. And can I have ²_____ mushrooms too, please? About half a kilo?
ASSISTANT	OK. Anything ³_____ ?
CUSTOMER	Oh, yes – tomatoes. A kilo of tomatoes, please. And ⁴_____ olives.
ASSISTANT	Sorry, we haven't got ⁵_____ olives today. Try the ⁶_____ across the street.
CUSTOMER	OK, thanks.
ASSISTANT	Here are your tomatoes. So, are you going to make pizza tonight with all this?
CUSTOMER	No, I'm not. I'm making '⁷_____ à la grecque'. It's a French dish. I had it on holiday in France. I loved it!
ASSISTANT	What about lemons? You don't ⁸_____ to put lemon juice in it, but it's a ⁹_____ good idea!
CUSTOMER	Oh, right. No, it's OK, thanks. I've ¹⁰_____ got lemons at home. So how ¹¹_____ is that?
ASSISTANT	Let's see. That's £4.35, please.
CUSTOMER	Here you are – £5.
ASSISTANT	And 65p ¹²_____ . Thanks. Enjoy your dinner!

2 **Complete each sentence with** *some* **or** *any*. **Then match the sentences with the pictures. Write the numbers 1–8.**

1 There's _____ yoghurt in the fridge.
2 There are _____ mushrooms in the kitchen.
3 There aren't _____ mushrooms in the pizza.
4 I'd like _____ of those potatoes, please.
5 Sorry, there aren't _____ potatoes.
6 I'd like _____ coffee, please.
7 Oh, there isn't _____ yoghurt.
8 No, I don't want _____ coffee, thanks.

3 **SPEAKING** **Which of these things would you always / never / sometimes see on a pizza?**

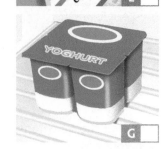

carrots | onions | peppers | yoghurt | pears
pineapple | chicken | mushrooms | tomatoes
cheese | olives

> There's always cheese on a
> pizza – but you never see ... !

4 **ROLE PLAY** **Work in pairs. Use your sentences from Exercise 3 to do a role play.**

In a restaurant

1 🔊 1.06 **Read the sentences. Mark them W (waitress) or C (customer). Listen and check.**

1 Can we see the menu, please?
2 Is everything OK?
3 There's too much salt in the soup!
4 The bill, please.
5 A table for two? This way, please.
6 We'd both like the fish, please. And the soup to start.
7 It's very noisy here. There are too many people.
8 Are you ready to order?

2 **Complete each phrase with** *much* **or** *many*.

1 too _____ sugar
2 too _____ salt
3 too _____ mushrooms
4 too _____ money
5 too _____ people
6 too _____ things on the menu

3 **Complete the mini-dialogues with a phrase from Exercise 2.**

1 A This soup is horrible.
  B I know! There's _____ in it.
2 A Ugh! I can't drink this coffee.
  B I know! There's _____ in it.
3 A This pizza isn't so good.
  B I know! I like mushrooms, but there are _____ on it!
4 A This is horrible. We can't talk.
  B I know! There are _____ here.
5 A I don't know what to choose.
  B I know! There are _____ .
6 A Look! €30.00 for a pizza!!
  B I know! It's _____ .

Shops

1 **Look at the shops below. What things can you buy in each place? Think of as many things as you can.**

newsagent's ☐   shoe shop ☐
chemist's ☐   post office ☐
bookshop ☐   supermarket ☐
clothes shop ☐   sports shop ☐

2 🔊 1.07 **Listen. Which shop is each person in? Write the number of the dialogue next to the correct shop in Exercise 1. There are three shops you won't need.**

3 🔊 1.07 **Listen again. In which shop do you hear these words?**

1 You don't have to wait in a queue. _____
2 You have to wear them two or three times. _____
3 You don't have to buy a larger size than you need. _____
4 You have to fill in this form. _____
5 You don't have to pay for the third one. _____

Things you have to do

1 **Read the sentences below. For each one, think of possibilities for a) who said it and b) who to.**

1 *You don't have to eat it.*
2 *You have to give it to me tomorrow morning.*
3 *I don't have to listen to you!*
4 *I have to finish this tonight.*
5 *You don't have to put mushrooms on it.*
6 *It's fantastic! I have to buy it!*

2 SPEAKING **Work in pairs. Choose three of the sentences in Exercise 1. Act out a mini-dialogue for each sentence that you choose.**

Chicken? Again? That's boring.

Well, you don't have to eat it.

Can I have something else?

No, we've only got chicken.

OK then – I'll eat the chicken.

Hi Susana

I was really happy to get your email saying that you're coming to visit us next weekend. It's great news, and you're going to be here at just the right time!

Next weekend our town is having its special weekend gala. There is one every year. What's a gala? Well, it's like a party but with sports and other events, too. There are lots of different activities. We're going to join in, so I hope you're ready for some fun!

It all starts on Saturday. There's an opening ceremony at lunchtime, and in the afternoon, there are things for kids – races and games and things. And at six o'clock there's a football match – our town team are playing against another town near here. Then in the evening, a local band is playing in the town square.

On Sunday morning there's a charity run – it's about eight kilometres. It starts in the park and goes past the railway station and through the main shopping area, then finishes at the park again. And guess what? I'm running in the race! (Would you like to run too? I think we can get you in – let me know asap, OK?) And on Sunday afternoon, there's a big street party with games and things. The weather forecast says it's going to be sunny, so I'm going to wear my new summer clothes.

So we're looking forward to seeing you here. Oh, I almost forgot! On Sunday evening we're having a party at our place for my sister's 18th birthday! We're going to make it a really special party. Please say you don't have to leave on Sunday evening!

Anyway, let me know more about your plans. When are you arriving on Friday?

See you soon,

Belinda

D LOOKING AHEAD
Plans and arrangements

1 **Read the email. Match the times and the events.**

1 Saturday lunchtime ▢
2 Saturday afternoon ▢
3 Saturday evening ▢
4 Sunday morning ▢
5 Sunday afternoon ▢
6 Sunday evening ▢

a kids' games and races
b party for Belinda's sister
c opening ceremony
d local band
e charity run
f street party

2 **Read the sentences. What do the underlined verbs express? Write A (arrangement) or I (intention).**

1 In the evening, a local band is playing in the town square. ▢
2 I'm running in the race. ▢
3 We're going to join in. ▢
4 I'm going to wear my new summer clothes. ▢
5 We're going to make it a really special party. ▢
6 We're having a party at our place. ▢

3 **Underline other examples of present continuous for arrangements in Belinda's email.**

4 SPEAKING **Work in pairs. Ask and answer questions about plans you have for next weekend.**

What are you doing on Saturday morning?

I'm going running. / I'm not doing anything. Why?

Sports and sport verbs

1 **Complete the table with the sports in the list.**

running | football | tennis | gymnastics
athletics | rock climbing | karate | skiing

play	do	go

2 SPEAKING **Work in pairs. Which sports do you do often / sometimes / never? Talk to your partner.**

I often go running, but I never do karate.

Travel plans

1 🔊 1.08 **Put the parts of the dialogue in order. Then listen and check.**

- [ ] A Great idea. OK, see you soon. We're going to have a lot of fun this weekend!
- [ ] A Oh dear, 5.30 is difficult for me. Is it OK if I don't meet you at the station?
- [1] A Hey, Susana. What time are you arriving on Friday?
- [ ] A Well, sometimes the train's late. If it's late, I'll meet you.
- [ ] B OK. As soon as the train leaves London, I'll send you a text message.
- [ ] B 5.30 – I'm going to catch the four o'clock train from London.
- [ ] B I know. It's going to be great!
- [ ] B Of course. I can take a taxi. No problem.

2 **Complete the sentences with the correct form of the verbs in brackets.**

1 If I _____ (miss) the train, I _____ (catch) the next one.
2 If the train _____ (arrive) late, I _____ (take) a taxi.
3 If there _____ (not be) any taxis, I _____ (walk) to your place.
4 I'll send you a text message when I _____ (get) to the station.
5 As soon as I _____ (get) to your place, we _____ (start) having a good time.
6 If we _____ (not have) a good time, I _____ (not visit) you again!

3 **Lola travelled a lot last year. Complete the sentences with the past simple of the verbs in the list.**

~~take~~ | catch | drive | fly | miss | ride

4 **Complete the sentences with *be going to* and the verbs in the list.**

visit | take | not visit | get up | try | buy

1 We don't like flying so we _____ a train.
2 I want to go to New York. I _____ my ticket online.
3 My plane leaves at 6.00, so I _____ very early tomorrow.
4 We'll only be in Paris for one day, so we _____ any museums.
5 When we're in London, we _____ my cousins.
6 We love Spanish food, so we _____ all the best restaurants in Madrid!

5 **Imagine you can take a holiday wherever you want, any time you want. Make notes about your plans:**

- where you're going to go
- where you're going to stay
- how long your holiday is going to be
- what you're going to do
- who you're going to go with
- what you're going to eat
- what time of year you're going to go

6 **SPEAKING** **Work in pairs. Ask and answer about the holiday you planned in Exercise 5.**

Where are you going to go on holiday?

New York. And I'm going to stay in an expensive hotel.

0 She _took_ a taxi in Paris.

1 She _____ the train in Munich.

2 She _____ the train in Vienna.

3 She _____ to Rome.

4 She _____ to Madrid.

5 She _____ a bike in Athens.

1 | AMAZING PEOPLE

1 _____

2 _____

3 _____

4 _____

READING

1 Look at the photos. What is your first impression of these people? What adjectives could you use to describe them?

caring | friendly | boring | serious | cheerful
funny | intelligent | cool | confident | easy-going

2 `SPEAKING` Discuss the photos in pairs.

> *He seems friendly.*

> *She looks like a cheerful person because she's smiling.*

3 `SPEAKING` Use the adjectives in Exercise 1 and other adjectives to describe people you know. Give reasons.

> *My brother is very easy-going. He doesn't get angry very often.*

4 Read the responses to an online survey quickly. Write the name of each person under the photos.

5 `1.09` Read and listen to the responses again. Mark the sentences T (true) or F (false). Correct the false information.

1 Mrs Marconi has a dangerous job. ___
2 She isn't very popular with Bia's friends. ___
3 Mr Donaldson has a problem controlling his students. ___
4 Jacob thinks Mr Donaldson will be famous one day. ___
5 Alex's grandmother is older than she looks. ___
6 Gwen thinks it's important to enjoy life. ___
7 Oliver's aunt had a car accident. ___
8 Oliver's uncle changed after the accident. ___

WHO

`Popular` `Recent`

DO YOU ADMIRE MOST?

Jackie, 14 ⭐ Sofia Marconi, my friend Bia's mum, is probably the most amazing person I know. She's also extremely **brave**. She's a wildlife photographer and she travels to some of the most dangerous places on Earth to take photos of the world's most endangered animals. She's just come back from Papua New Guinea. I haven't seen her photos yet, but I bet they're amazing. She's quite famous and she's already been on TV. Although she spends quite a bit of time away from home, she's also a really cool mum. She's really **charming** and all of Bia's friends think she's fab. Bia's really lucky to have such a great mum.

Jacob, 16 One of my heroes is Mr Donaldson, our music teacher. First of all, he's a brilliant teacher. He's really **laid-back** but we all respect him, and no one ever messes about in his class. He's so **creative** and finds different ways to get us interested in his lessons. He's also a really amazing guitar player – I mean he is seriously **talented**. He's in a band. They haven't made any recordings yet, but they've already attracted lots of interest and I'm sure they're going to be famous one day. I'll be really happy for him, but I hope it doesn't happen too soon. I don't want to lose my teacher!

Alex, 15 The person I admire more than anyone is my grandmother Gwen. She's 78 and looks just amazing. Many people think she's my mother when they see us together. But she doesn't just *look* young, she *is* young. She's one of the most **active** people I know. She spends a lot of her time doing things for charity. For example, she's just done a parachute jump to raise money for a children's charity in India. A parachute jump! At her age! She's such a **positive** person, always seeing the good in other people. 'Life is for living,' she tells me. I hope I have that much life in me when I'm her age.

Oliver, 17 ⭐ The greatest person I know is my uncle Jack. He and my aunt Alice had the perfect life: good jobs, a lovely house and three young children. Then one day their life changed forever. My aunt had a terrible car accident. It left her in a wheelchair. From that day on, my uncle has devoted his time to looking after her and the family. But I have never heard him complain. He's still the same lovely person he always was. I know life is hard for him but he's always so **cheerful** with a huge smile on his face. He's such a **warm** person – someone you want to spend time with.

6 **VOCABULARY** **There are eight words in bold in the texts. Match the words with these meanings. Write the words.**

0 is always doing things _active_
1 is usually happy _____
2 is very easy-going _____
3 has very original ideas _____
4 looks for the good in all situations

   _____

5 is very good at doing something

   _____

6 doesn't get scared easily _____
7 is very easy to like _____

7 **Complete the sentences with the words from Exercise 6.**

0 Why are you so _cheerful_ today? Have you had some good news?
1 He stood up in the front of the whole school and read out his poem. He was really _____ .
2 She's very _____ and it's easy to see why she's got so many friends.
3 He's so _____ that some people think he's a bit lazy.
4 Have you seen him doing ballet? He really is a _____ dancer.
5 If you want to work in advertising, you need to be _____ and come up with really good ideas.
6 My dad is really _____ around the house. He's always cooking or fixing things or working in the garden.
7 He's had a really difficult life but he's really _____ about the future.

■ THiNK VALUES ■

Human qualities

1 **Think about someone who is not famous but who you think is special.**

a Think of three adjectives to describe them.

b Think about why you chose these adjectives. Make notes.

2 **SPEAKING** **Tell your partner about the person you admire.**

> *I really admire my brother. He's really confident in difficult situations.*

GRAMMAR

Present perfect with *just*, *already* and *yet*

1 Complete the example sentences with *just*, *already* and *yet*. Then complete the rules with the missing words.

1 She's _____ come back from Papua New Guinea.

2 They haven't made any recordings _____ , but they've _____ attracted a lot of interest.

> **RULE:** In the present perfect, we often use
>
> - ^{1}_____ in negative sentences and questions to talk about something that hasn't happened but that we expect to happen soon. It comes at the end of the sentence.
> - ^{2}_____ to emphasise that something happened very recently. It goes before the past participle.
> - ^{3}_____ to show that something has been done or finished sooner than expected. It usually goes before the past participle.

2 Match the pictures and the sentences. Write 1–3 in the boxes.

1 He's just finished his painting.

2 He's already sold the painting.

3 He hasn't finished his painting yet.

3 Look at Mike's list of things to do for his party. Write sentences with *already* and *yet*.

Party list – things to do
1 make cake
✓ 2 send out invitations
3 organise music
✓ 4 choose what to wear
5 decorate room
✓ 6 buy drinks

1 *He hasn't made the cake yet.*

4 Use your imagination to answer the questions. Use the present perfect and *just* in each one.

1 Why is Mum so angry?
   Because Dad's just crashed her car.

2 Why is Colin so sad?

3 Why is your face so dirty?

4 What's Liam so scared about?

5 Why is Dana so excited?

6 Why are you smiling?

5 Tick (✓) the things you have already done.

Eight things to do before you're 20

- start a blog
- meet a famous person
- travel abroad
- write a song
- act on stage
- learn a musical instrument
- enter a competition
- climb a mountain

6 SPEAKING Work in pairs. Ask each other questions.

Have you started a blog yet?

Yes, I've already done that. Have you?

No, I haven't done that yet.

Workbook page 10

LISTENING

1 ◀》 1.10 **Listen to some people playing a game called Mystery Guest. How many people are playing?**

2 ◀》 1.10 **Listen again. For each question there are three pictures. Choose the correct picture and put a tick (✓) in the box below it.**

1 What does Will's mystery guest do?

A ☐   B ☐   C ☐

2 Where is Will's mystery guest from?

A ☐   B ☐   C ☐

3 Who does Will think Kiki's mystery guest is?

A ☐   B ☐   C ☐

4 What does Kiki's mystery guest do?

A ☐   B ☐   C ☐

3 ◀》 1.10 **Work in pairs. Answer the questions. Then listen again and check.**

1 Who is Will's mystery guest?
2 What adjectives does Will use to describe him?
3 Who is Kiki's mystery guest?
4 What adjectives does Kiki use to describe her?

4 SPEAKING **Work in pairs. Play Mystery Guest.**

> *Ladies and gentlemen, my guest is …*

> *He/She has won / played / recorded / helped …*

■ THiNK SELF-ESTEEM ■

Personal qualities

1 A cinquain is a short, five-line poem. Read the cinquain and complete the rules with the words in the list.

Kiki

Charming, creative

Sings – laughs – loves

Talented

A beautiful voice

adjectives | three | verbs
someone's name | adjective

On the first line write ¹_____ .
On the second line write two ²_____ to describe the person.
On the third line write three ³_____ to show what the person likes doing.
On the fourth line write another ⁴_____ .
On the fifth line write a description of the person in just ⁵_____ words.

2 WRITING **Write a cinquain about:**

a your partner or best friend
b your hero

READING

1 SPEAKING **Work in pairs. At what age did you learn to do these things?**

- read
- draw
- play a musical instrument
- speak a foreign language

> *I learned to read when I was ...*

> *I've never learned to ...*

2 SPEAKING **What other things have you learned in your life and when did you start to do them?**

> *When I was seven I learned how to cook an omelette.*

3 **Read the TV programme preview quickly. Which of the children is a genius at these things? Write the names.**

1 art _____
2 music _____
3 creative writing _____
4 languages _____

4 **Read the programme preview again and answer the questions.**

1 What writers did Mark enjoy when he was three?
2 What languages does he know?
3 How much will Daniel get for writing each book?
4 How many instruments does Samantha play?
5 How many weeks is the show on for?
6 Who will the show have interviews with?

Don't miss this week:

Britain's Smartest Kids

While other children were just starting their ABCs, three-year-old Mark Swallow was already reading Shakespeare and Charles Dickens. By the age of seven he was speaking fluent French and German and studying both Latin and Greek. Now, at the age of 12, Mark has just started a university degree in English literature.

Mark and other child geniuses will be the subject of a new documentary series which takes a look into the lives of these remarkable children and their families. In the programmes we will meet children like eight-year-old Daniel Manning, who wrote his first book when he was just five and who has just signed a £60,000 contract with a publishing house to write three novels. Then there is 12-year-old Samantha Price, who started piano lessons when she was three. Along with the piano, she now also plays the cello, clarinet and classical guitar. She has already played with three top European orchestras. And how about ten-year-old Jordan Welsh? She first picked up a paint brush before she could walk. She has already had an exhibition of her paintings in one of London's top art galleries and has just won a major prize for one of her paintings.

Over the next six weeks we will see what it is that makes these children so special. We will find out how and when their parents knew they were different and about the changes it made to their family life. We will hear from the children about their hopes and plans for the future. There are also interviews with former child geniuses, some who have gone on to great things and others who decided they wanted to return to a more normal life.

Join us Monday for the first documentary in this amazing series, **Britain's Smartest Kids.**

GRAMMAR
Present perfect vs. past simple

1 Look back at the review on page 16. Which questions can you answer with a specific point in time? Then complete the rules with *present perfect* or *past simple*.

1 When did Daniel write his first book?
2 When did he sign a £60,000 contract?
3 When did Samantha start piano lessons?
4 When did she play with orchestras?

> **RULE:** When we talk about a specific point in time in the past, we use the _____ .
> When we don't refer to a specific point in time, we often use the _____ .

2 Complete the pairs of sentences. Use the past simple and the present perfect of the verbs.

0 visit
  a I _have visited_ Greece more than 20 times.
  b I first _visited_ Greece in 1998.
1 win
  a He _____ already _____ three gold medals, and he hopes to win more.
  b He _____ a gold medal in the 2012 Olympics.
2 meet
  a My mum _____ a lot of interesting people in her life.
  b My mum _____ Prince Harry ten years ago.
3 do
  a Mum, I _____ my homework. Can I go out?
  b I _____ all the things on my to-do list before lunch!
4 record
  a They _____ their last album two years ago.
  b They _____ more than 20 albums so far.
5 live
  a We _____ in Samoa for three years when I was a teenager.
  b We're living in Austria now, but we _____ in many different countries.
6 sign
  a She _____ just _____ a contract with a new e-publishing company.
  b She _____ the contract for her first book on her 16th birthday.

Workbook page 11

VOCABULARY
Collocations

1 Circle all the correct answers.

1 Which of these can you sign?
  a a contract   b an autograph   c a lesson
2 Which of these things can you write?
  a a novel   b a party   c a song
3 Which of these things can you do?
  a a good time   b a degree   c something
4 Which of these things can you win?
  a a prize   b a competition   c an exhibition
5 Which of these can you make?
  a friends   b a cake   c homework
6 Which of these can you miss?
  a a future   b your family   c the bus

2 What verbs can go before the six words you didn't circle in Exercise 1? Write at least one verb for each word.

3 **SPEAKING** Talk to other people in the class. Ask and answer questions and complete the table.

> Have you ever … ? What happened?

> What was the poem about?

> Who did you ask?

> What did you win?

Find someone who has …	Who?	Details
asked someone for an autograph.		
written a poem.		
had an interview.		
won a prize.		
made a cake.		
missed a train or a bus.		

Workbook page 12

WRITING

Write a short passage about someone you have admired for some time. Include

- how long you have known them.
- what you admire about them.

The new café

1 Look at the photos and answer the questions.

There is going to be a new café in the park.
Who does Luke think should open it?
Who does Ryan think should open it?

2 🔊 1.11 Now read and listen to the photostory. Check your answers.

1

LUKE Have you read this? They're opening a new café in the park. Saturday afternoon.
OLIVIA That's fantastic. Who's going to do the big opening ceremony?
RYAN The mayor probably. She always does shop openings and conferences, that sort of thing.
MEGAN They should get somebody more important.
LUKE What? More important than the mayor?

2

LUKE Hey, I know. They should get Paul Norris.
RYAN Yeah! He's a great footballer! He plays for United now, but he grew up round here.
OLIVIA But he doesn't live round here any more. He's a big star now. Let's face it, he won't want to open a little park café.
RYAN Yeah, you're probably right.

3

RYAN What about Paula Mayberry?
OLIVIA The actress from the soap opera, what's it called … Linden Street?
RYAN Yes.
MEGAN But why her? Did she live here once?
RYAN No, I don't think so. I'd just like to meet her.

4

LUKE Come on, there has to be somebody!
OLIVIA Look, the mayor is going to open the park café, and that's that.
RYAN I guess you're right. No one special lives in our town.
MEGAN Are you sure?
LUKE What do you mean?
MEGAN Know what, guys? I've just thought of someone *very* special, and he's just the person for the job.

DEVELOPING SPEAKING

3 Work in pairs. Discuss what happens next in the story. Write down your ideas.

We think the boys go and talk to Paul Norris, the footballer.

4 ▶ EP1 Watch to find out how the story continues.

5 Complete the sentences with the words in the list.

Megan | the headmaster | the girls | Mr Lane
Olivia | the boys | the girls

1 Megan doesn't tell her idea to _____ .
2 Megan shares her idea with _____ .
3 Olivia offers to help _____ .
4 The girls go to see _____ .
5 The boys follow _____ .
6 The mayor thanks. _____ .
7 Olivia's special person is. _____ .

PHRASES FOR FLUENCY

1 Find the expressions 1–6 in the story. Who says them? How do you say them in your language?

1 … that sort of thing.   *Ryan*
2 Let's face it, …   _____
3 I don't think so.   _____
4 … and that's that.   _____
5 Are you sure?   _____
6 Know what?   _____

2 Complete the conversations with the expressions in Exercise 1.

1 **A** That new girl, Sally – she likes you!
  B No, [1]_____ .
  A [2]_____ ? I have a feeling she likes you a lot.
  B No. She never smiles at me. And she criticises me a lot, doesn't laugh at my jokes, [3]_____ .
2 **A** Oh, you got it wrong again!
  B I know. [4]_____ , I'm no good at computer games.
  A [5]_____ ? We just need a rest. Let's go and watch some TV.
  B OK, but I don't want to play this game again, OK? I'm useless at it, [6]_____ !

Pronunciation
Intonation and sentence stress
Go to page 120. 🔊

WordWise
Phrases with *just*

1 Look at the sentences from the unit. Choose the correct meaning of *just* in each one.

1 She's **just** come back from Papua New Guinea. ☐
2 He wrote his first book when he was **just** five. ☐
3 She's 78 and looks **just** amazing. ☐

a only
b a short time ago
c really

2 What does *just* mean in these sentences?

1 Don't be angry. It's just a joke.
2 I've just seen a fantastic film.
3 It's cold today. The weather is just awful.
4 No food, thanks – just a drink.
5 She's just had some bad news.

3 Match the questions to the answers.

1 How many spoons of sugar would you like? ☐
2 When did Jane get here? ☐
3 What do you think of Beyoncé? ☐

a She's just arrived.
b She's just great.
c Just one   ► Workbook page 13

FUNCTIONS
Offering encouragement

1 ▶ EP1 Watch the video again. Listen for sentences 1–5. Who says them? Why?

1 That is a great idea.
2 You should definitely do it.
3 You've got to make this happen.
4 I'll help you if you want.
5 Let's go and speak to some people.

Good causes

2 ROLE PLAY Work in pairs. Student A: go to page 127. Student B: go to page 128. Use the sentences from Exercise 1 to do the role play.

OBJECTIVES

FUNCTIONS: asking and giving / refusing permission to do something

GRAMMAR: present perfect with *for* and *since*; *a, an, the* or no article

VOCABULARY: school subjects; verbs about thinking

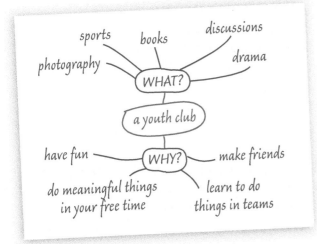

2 Look at the photos. What are the people doing? Where do you think they are?

3 🔊 1.14 Read and listen to the article. For each question, mark the correct letter A, B, C or D.

1 What is the writer doing in this text?
   A Describing a summer school he started in 2005.
   B Explaining how to send a child to Tinkering.
   C Talking about the US school system.
   D Talking about G. Tulley's programmes for kids.

2 What does the text say about safety at the school?
   A The school is too dangerous for kids.
   B No child has ever had an accident.
   C Children have never hurt themselves badly.
   D The school doesn't give information about that.

3 What reactions to Brightworks have there been in the media?
   A They have compared it to Tinkering School.
   B Most of them have been positive.
   C There hasn't been any reaction.
   D Most of them have been negative.

4 What effect has the school had on Tina Cooper?
   A It has changed her opinion about school.
   B It has given her exciting and boring times.
   C It has made her more interested in San Francisco.
   D It has encouraged her to ask more questions.

4 Which thing might Gever Tulley say in a presentation to parents about the Tinkering School?

A We are trying to do our best. We offer your kids a balance of things they will like doing and things they will have to do.

B I can guarantee that your son or daughter will learn to build a rollercoaster, a rope bridge, a tree house, a motorbike and a boat.

C Kids can learn a lot by doing things in teams. We give them materials and tools. They plan and make things.

D Most of the articles in newspapers and magazines say kids are more motivated here than at many other schools.

READING

1 Work in pairs. Write down words that come to mind when you think of these places.

a youth club | a holiday camp | a school

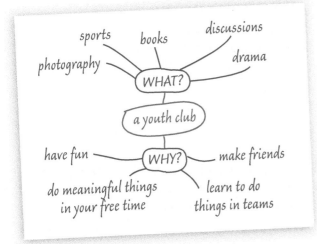

An education like no other

Gever Tulley is a computer scientist from California. In 2005, he started a summer programme for children called Tinkering School. The idea was that children can learn important skills for life by building things together. Gever Tulley and his team help the children to think big and create plans for innovative things they want to build. Children have made fantastic things since the school started. They have built a rollercoaster. They have made a rope bridge from plastic shopping bags. They have made tree houses, wooden motorbikes and boats.

At Tinkering School, children get all kinds of materials like wood, metal, plastic, nails and ropes. They get lots of real tools too, such as knives, hammers, screwdrivers and power drills. Some children have cut themselves when using a knife, or hurt their fingers when using a hammer. Tinkering School has been around for many years now, but nobody has ever suffered a serious injury in all those years. This is because there are strict health and safety regulations they must follow. The children always learn how to use the tools safely and they must wear the right clothing and protection at all times.

Gever Tulley's ideas have worked very well. A lot of children have gone to his summer schools over the years. In 2011, Gever Tulley and a colleague decided to create a 'real' school, called Brightworks, in San Francisco. The school is

very small – it only has 20 students aged 6 to 13. Brightworks is based on the same principles as Tinkering School.

Since it started, Brightworks has been written about a lot. Most of those articles have been very positive. They have praised the quality of the school. They have found the children are more motivated than at many other schools. But since the beginning of the school there have also been critical voices. Some people have said that children are not learning enough at Brightworks. They feel that students and teachers are just 'playing around' all the time.

The students at Brightworks seem to love their school. We spoke to 12-year-old Tina Cooper. She has been a student at the school since last October. 'Since I started here, I've never sat in a 'normal' class with a teacher,' she told us. 'But it's been a very exciting experience. I've worked hard at my new school for eight months now, and there hasn't been one single moment when I found it boring. Before, I was bored quite often.'

▉ THiNK VALUES ▉

Learning for life

1 **Read the statements. Tick (✓) the things that you think kids are likely to learn at Tinkering School and Brightworks.**

☐ Everyone is different and that's a good thing.

☐ Teamwork is important to achieve things in life.

☐ When you use a tool you have to be careful.

☐ It is important to be friendly and help others.

☐ It is very important in life to eat healthy food.

☐ Mistakes are important. We learn from them.

2 SPEAKING **Compare your ideas with a partner.**

> I think they learn how to be careful with tools.

> Why?

> The text says there are strict health and safety regulations.

> Yes, I agree with you.

3 SPEAKING **Discuss these questions.**

1 Which of the things from the list above do you think are important to learn?

2 What would you add to your personal list of 'Important things to learn'?

GRAMMAR
Present perfect with *for* and *since*

1 Look back at the article on page 21. <u>Underline</u> all the sentences in the present perfect.

2 Complete the sentences below with *for* and *since*. Then complete the rules.

  1 Children have made fantastic things _____ the school started.

  2 Tinkering School has been around _____ many years now.

> RULE: In the present perfect, we use
> - ¹_____ to talk about a period of time.
> - ²_____ to refer to the point in time when an action started.

3 When do we use *for* and when do we use *since*? Complete the chart with the words and phrases in the list.

~~a month~~ | ~~last summer~~ | your birthday | yesterday
a year | 2014 | I phoned you | a long time
many years | days | Friday | an hour

for	*a month*	_____	_____
	_____	_____	_____
since	*last summer*	_____	_____
	_____	_____	_____

4 Complete the sentences. Use the present perfect form of the verbs and *for* or *since*.

  1 I _____ (be) at my new school _____ last December.

  2 Hilary _____ (not see) Michael _____ several weeks.

  3 They _____ (not write) an email or _____ (phone) us _____ three months.

  4 He _____ (live) in this town _____ a long time.

  5 I _____ (have) this camera _____ I was 10.

5 Write sentences using the present perfect with *for* or *since*.

  0 Rebecca doesn't live in Italy now. (three years)
    Rebecca hasn't lived in Italy for three years.

  1 They are in the youth club. (three hours)

  2 Joanne and I are good friends. (primary school)

  3 She plays in the volleyball team. (two months)

  4 I ought to see a doctor. I am sick. (a week)

  5 I don't hear a lot from Sandra. (last October)

Workbook page 18 ▶

VOCABULARY
School subjects

1 🔊 1.15 Match the school subjects in the list with the photos. Write 1–12 in the boxes. Then listen and check.

  1 Science (Physics, Biology and Chemistry)
  2 Music | 3 Art Education | 4 Drama
  5 Design and Technology | 6 Geography
  7 English | 8 PE (Physical Education)
  9 ICT (Information and Communication Technology)
  10 Maths | 11 History | 12 Spanish

2 SPEAKING Answer the questions. Take notes. Then compare your answers with a partner.

  1 Which are your favourite subjects? Which don't you like? Why?

  2 Which of the subjects are you studying this year?

  3 How long have you studied each subject?

Workbook page 20 ▶

LISTENING

1 Work in pairs. Match the activities with the photos.

1 make a fire | 2 spend a night outdoors | 3 climb a tree | 4 drive a car | 5 spend an hour blindfolded

2 SPEAKING Which of these things have you done? Tell your partner.

3 ◀》 1.16 Listen to David talking about a book his father has just read. Which of the activities in Exercise 1 do they talk about?

4 ◀》 1.16 Listen again. Mark the sentences T (true) or F (false).

1 David is babysitting his little brother. ___

2 David thinks the book his father read is nonsense. ___

3 The book says children should spend an hour blindfolded alone. ___

4 David is not sure his dad will let Nick drive a car. ___

5 Nick drove the car straight into a tree. ___

6 David thinks Nick will enjoy showing that he can make a fire. ___

FUNCTIONS
Asking and giving / refusing permission

1 Put the dialogues into the correct order. Write the numbers 1–4.

	DAD	Yes?
	DAD	I'm afraid I need it myself right now.
	NICK	Will you let me use your laptop?
	NICK	Dad?

	ANNIE	Can I watch the football match tonight?
	ANNIE	Can I ask you something, Mum?
	MUM	Yes, of course you can.
	MUM	Go ahead.

2 Mark the sentences *AP* (asking permission), *GP* (giving permission) or *RP* (refusing permission).

1 Will you let me use your camera? _____
Yeah, sure. Of course I will. _____

2 Can I borrow your bike? _____
No, sorry. I need it. _____

3 Can I use your laptop? _____
Yes, you can, but I want it back tomorrow.
_____

4 Is it OK if I borrow this necklace? _____
Yeah, but be really careful with it, OK?

3 ROLE PLAY Work in pairs. Act out short conversations. Ask each other for permission. You can use the ideas here or come up with your own.

use his/her tablet | come with him/her borrow £20 | copy his/her homework get some help with homework

READING

1 **Look at this picture. Think about the questions and compare your answers with a partner.**

1 What does the picture show?
2 Where in the picture is the brain?
3 What does the brain do?

Learning is brain change

(1) Everybody has a brain, but not many people know how the brain works. Some people believe that the brain is like the hard disk of a computer. We use it to store files – images, language (words, texts, sounds) and other data. Others compare the brain to a huge container or cupboard with lots of little drawers, shelves and boxes in it. We put information into these boxes and hope to find it again later.

(2) The brain is not a computer disk, and it isn't a container. Look at the picture here. It looks a bit like weeds in a garden, doesn't it? The picture actually shows a child's neocortex – a part of the brain. You can guess what happens – more 'weeds' grow as the child gets older. Scientists call these neuronal networks. The networks grow around our neurons,

or nerve cells. What makes them grow? Learning! 'Learning is brain change,' says Professor James Zull from Case Western University in Cleveland, Ohio, USA. 'Without learning, nothing changes in the brain. For every new word you learn in your English lesson, every puzzle you solve in maths, every new song you learn to sing, a neuronal network grows in your brain and the brain changes.'

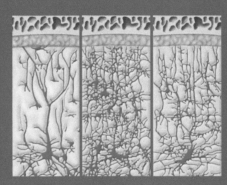

(3) The more neuronal networks we grow, the better we can think and the better we remember. You may wonder if there is anything you can do to make the networks in your brain grow better. Professor Zull says yes, there is. He says that brain change is strongest when a) you are interested in and like what you are learning, b) you are in control of what you learn and c) you get challenging tasks that make you think hard and concentrate. Understanding a challenging task makes you feel good and develops your brain!

Neuronal networks at 9 months, 2 years and 4 years of age

2 **Match the words with the meanings. Write the numbers 1–5. Then read the text to check your answers.**

1 to store │ 2 a container │ 3 a weed
4 a nerve cell │ 5 ~~to concentrate~~

a to think very carefully about what you are doing — [5]
b to keep things for use in the future — [ ]
c a wild plant that grows in a garden — [ ]
d it carries information between the brain and the body — [ ]
e an object used to carry or store things — [ ]

3 **Read the text again. Mark the sentences T (true) or F (false).**

1 The text compares the brain to weeds. ___
2 The brain is a system of neuronal networks that can change. ___
3 Whenever we learn anything, a change happens in our brain. ___
4 We can't really make our brain stronger. ___
5 Being able to do difficult tasks is good for the brain. ___

▮ TRAIN TO THINK ▮
Learning about texts

1 **Choose the best description of this text.**

A an adventure story to entertain the reader.
B an ad to sell the reader something.
C a magazine article to give the reader information.
D a letter to persuade the reader to do something.

2 **Choose the title that best sums up the content of each paragraph. There is one extra title.**

A The brain – a fantastic computer ___
B What people believe about the brain ___
C How to make your brain stronger ___
D Our brain is a growing system ___

GRAMMAR
a, *an*, *the* or no article

1 Look at the sentences from a magazine article. <u>Underline</u> *a*, *an*, *the* and the nouns these articles are with. Then go through the sentences again and (circle) the nouns with no article. Finally complete the rule with *a*, *an*, *the*, – (no article).

> Food is important for your body. But did you know that the food you eat is important for your brain, too? Here is an example: sugar. Sugar tastes good. But the sugar from sweets can create problems. Your concentration and your memory get worse. What can we learn from the example here? It's better to eat an orange or a banana than to eat chocolate, because that's good for your brain and for your body.

> **RULE:** We use
>
> • _____ or _____ + a singular countable noun when the listener/reader doesn't know exactly which thing we are talking about.
>   *You can have **an apple** or **a banana**.*
>   *We've got **a new car**.*
>
> • _____ + noun when it is clear which thing(s) or person/people we are talking about.
>   *The **apples in this pie** are from our garden.*
>   *The **bananas that I bought** yesterday are horrible.*
>
> • _____ + plural countable noun or + uncountable noun, when we are talking about things in general.
>   ***Bananas** are sweeter than **apples**. **Chocolate** isn't good for you.*

2 Complete each sentence with *a*, *an*, *the* or – (no article).

0 She is ___*a*___ good student.

1 She eats a lot of _____ fruit and _____ vegetables.

2 _____ book that you gave me was really good.

3 I have _____ idea. Let's watch _____ new Beyoncé video.

4 I never drink _____ coffee – I hate it.

5 I like lots of sports, but _____ sport I like most is _____ tennis.

3 Complete the text with *a*, *an*, *the* or –.

⁰ — People need to drink. Of course ¹_____ orange juice and ²_____ apple juice are very popular, but they are not always ³_____ good choice. ⁴_____ orange juice has got a lot of sugar in it, so don't drink too much of it. The best drink for your brain is ⁵_____ water. ⁶_____ glass of water is the best drink you can get, but ⁷_____ water that you drink needs to be fresh and clean.

Workbook page 19

VOCABULARY
Verbs about thinking

1 Use a dictionary to make sure you know the meaning of these words.

to concentrate on | to remember | to think
to imagine | to wonder | to believe
to guess | to recognise | to realise
to suppose

2 Choose the correct words.

1 The task was very difficult. I had to *remember* / *think* for a long time.

2 Come on, don't be silly. I don't *believe* / *realise* in ghosts!

3 Can you *imagine* / *concentrate* how great it must be to live at the beach?

4 When the teacher asked the question a different way, I *supposed* / *realised* that I knew the answer!

5 Did they really say they are moving to New York? I don't *suppose* / *believe* it!

6 I have not seen her for six years. I don't think I would *realise* / *recognise* her.

7 I have no idea what the answer is. I'll just have to *imagine* / *guess*.

8 I was so tired that I found it hard to *think* / *concentrate on* the test.

9 Have you ever *wondered* / *supposed* why I haven't phoned you for months?

10 If we want to get there faster, I *wonder* / *suppose* we should take a taxi.

> **Pronunciation**
> Word stress
> **Go to page 120.**

3 **SPEAKING** Work in pairs. Ask and answer questions.

1 Are there any places where you can think really well or not well at all?

2 Does music help you to concentrate or make it difficult for you to concentrate? Does it matter what kind of music it is?

3 In what situations can you imagine things really well? Do you find it difficult to use your imagination sometimes?

4 Do you find it difficult to remember things sometimes? What sort of things?

5 Do you believe in life on other planets? What do you suppose the people there look like?

Workbook page 20

Culture

A day in the life of ...

1 🔊 1.19 **Look at the photos. What do you think a typical day for a student at each of these three schools is like? Read and listen to check.**

1 Alexander, student at a Dance Academy in Moscow, Russia

I've been at this dance Academy for three years. This is a typical day for me:

I get up around eight o'clock, have a quick breakfast, do my hair, and get into my dance clothes. I arrive at the school around 8.45, just in time for the warm-up before class.

My first class, classical ballet, starts at 9.00 and finishes at 10.30. I then have a 20-minute break. I eat a banana on the way to another building. As soon as I arrive there, my modern dance class starts. It runs until 12.15. Then I have a 45-minute lunch break. In the afternoon it's classical ballet again, then gymnastics to strengthen the muscles. I get home around seven, and I'm usually very tired.

On Saturdays, I only have a one-and-a-half-hour ballet class, and on Sundays I'm free.

2 Ethan, college basketball player from Chicago, USA

My day starts at 8 am with the weight training program. We do a ten-minute warm-up, and then it's hard work for 50 minutes.

At nine o'clock my classes start. When we have an away match, we can't do so much school work. When we are back at school, we have to work harder than the others. But I'm not complaining – I've been in the team for more than a year now, and it's cool.

I have a break between 1.00 and 2.30. I try to take only 30 minutes for lunch and the rest I use for studying. The afternoon is full of classes and practice.

At night I have to watch videos of games, I have to read books about basketball and study for my exams, too. When I finally go to bed – often nearly midnight – I'm completely exhausted!

3 Ella, drama student from Sydney, Australia

6.45: I'm not good at getting up early. Three alarm clocks – at 6.30, 6.40 and 6.50.

8.00: Voice training. Important for an actor.

8.45: Gymnastics – I like it. It helps me concentrate better and makes me feel good.

9.30: Singing and dance workshop. It's hard work, but it gives me energy. Music and rhythm. Love it!

11.00: First break – drink, drink, drink – water, of course. No drinks with sugar in them. Makes the body and the mind tired.

11.15: Performance workshop. Hard work. Our teachers are fantastic, but they tell you when you make mistakes!

12.30: Lunch break – I eat nuts and fruit, or a salad at one of the cafés nearby. I never eat carbohydrates, you know, pasta or other heavy stuff.

2.00: A lecture about acting, for example, how to move on the stage, what to do with your hands, etc. Not always easy to concentrate after lunch.

3.30: Short break. I try not to fall asleep. The day has been very tiring!

3.45: Voice training workshop, dance and singing.

6.00: Evening rehearsal. We practise for a performance at the end of term. We're doing a musical this term. Hard work and great fun.

9.00: I go home.

10.00: Zzzz!

2 Read the article again. Complete the sentences with *Alexander*, *Ethan* or *Ella*.

1 _____ often studies for many hours at night.

2 _____ knows very well what to eat and what to drink.

3 _____'s life is more relaxed at weekends.

4 _____ is free in the evenings.

5 _____ learns about body language.

6 _____ accepts that other students sometimes have to work less.

3 VOCABULARY Read the article again. Find words or phrases with the following meaning.

1 make my hair look good (story 1) *do my hair*

2 gentle exercises you do before doing a sport to prepare your body (story 1) _____

3 a very traditional type of dancing (story 1) _____

4 to make something stronger (story 1) _____

5 exercise that makes the muscles stronger (story 2) _____

6 a match that a team plays at the sports ground of the other team (story 2) _____

7 almost midnight (story 2) _____

8 extremely tired (story 2) _____

9 a formal talk given to a group of students (story 3) _____

10 food such as bread, potatoes or rice (story 3) _____

11 a type of lesson where you learn something practical (story 3) _____

12 the action of entertaining other people by dancing, singing, etc. (story 3) _____

WRITING
An email describing your school routine

1 Read this email from your friend in Cambridge. Then answer the questions.

1 How does Kylie feel about her new class?

2 What does Kylie think of Luca and why?

3 Does Kylie think you've gozvt less school work than her?

4 How does her work for school compare to last year?

5 What subject does she get a lot of homework for, and how does she feel about it?

2 Underline sentences in the email where Kylie writes about these things. What tense does she use in the sentences you underlined? Why does she use it?

a asks how you feel about your new school

b talks about Luca's father

c compares school this year to last year

d talks about the amount of homework this year

3 Put the words in the right order. Write the sentences. What tense are they in and why?

1 new / too / class / kid / There's / a / my / in

_____

2 a week / at / four times / come home / 5.30 / I

_____

3 love / projects / I / class / But / the / do / this / in / we

_____

4 Match the four paragraphs of Kylie's email with the content.

Paragraph 1   a Kylie's new class
Paragraph 2   b a request to write soon
Paragraph 3   c an introduction
Paragraph 4   d work this year compared to last

5 Read Kylie's email again. Make notes with your own ideas on how:

a to answer the question in her introduction

b to describe your new class (new school? classmates?)

c to compare your work this year to last year's

d to say how you feel about your subjects (any subjects you particularly like/don't like? Why?)

e you could finish your email (What do you want to know from Kylie?)

6 Write an email to Kylie (about 200 words). Look at your notes from Exercise 5 and make sure you include all your ideas. Make sure you use the present continuous when necessary.

Hi there!

I hope this finds you well. I haven't heard from you since the beginning of the holidays. Are you enjoying your new school?

I am, big time! I'm in a class with all my friends again – Emily, Kate, James and all the others. There's a new kid in my class too. His name's Luca and he's from Bologna in Italy. His father is working in the UK for a year, and the whole family have come over. He's cool. We have lots of fun together.

But of course, it's not all fun. We've got important exams this year so there's a lot of work to do. I'm spending more time at school than last year, and I come home at 5.30 four times a week. We're also getting a lot more homework, especially for Technology and Design. But I love the projects we do in this class!

Well, I guess it's not so different for you. If you've got a bit of time, please let me know how things are going. I'd really like to know what life at school is like for you. And remember, please, you've got a friend in Cambridge who would really like to get mail from you more often!

Write soon!

Kylie

■ THiNK EXAMS ■

READING
Part 3: True/false

1 **Look at the sentences. Read the text below to decide if each sentence is correct or incorrect. If it is correct, tick (✓) the box under A. If it is incorrect, tick (✓) the box under B.**

                                                                 A   B

1 The Tan-y-Bryn Outdoor Adventure Centre gets visitors from many different European countries.

2 Children learn about the countryside from books there.

3 The Centre is only open to school children.

4 The Centre offers three meals a day.

5 No one has been badly hurt during activities at the Centre.

6 The Centre will send people to talk to your family if you are interested in going.

Tan-y-Bryn Outdoor Adventure Centre

Since opening our doors in 1975, Tan-y-Bryn Outdoor Centre has welcomed thousands of young people from all over the UK to enjoy fun, education and adventure in the beautiful Welsh countryside. Whether they are climbing on the slopes of Mount Snowdon, snorkelling in the Menai Straits or birdwatching in the woodlands, our visitors enjoy hands-on experiences they will never forget.

For school groups, youth clubs and families we offer comfortable accommodation for up to 50 children and 10 adults. We also provide a full breakfast, lunch and dinner to make sure no one goes hungry. Safety is a top priority – there has never been a serious accident at the Centre.

Where are we? On the island of Anglesey in North Wales. By car, take the A4080 and follow the signs for Dwyran and then the Centre.

What do we offer? Outdoor activities – mountain biking, trail walking, geocaching, canoeing – as well as sports – everything from archery to tennis and football.

How do I find out more? Email us. For large bookings, a representative can visit your school or youth club to answer questions.

LISTENING
Part 1: Multiple choice

2 🔊 **1.20** **For each question, there are three pictures and a short recording. Choose the correct picture and put a tick (✓) in the box below it.**

1 What did Sally buy at the shops?

    A   B   C

2 What time is it?

    A   B   C

3 How did Brian get to work?

    A   B   C

4 Which lesson did Fred enjoy most?

    A   B   C

5 When is Tom's brother's birthday?

    A   B   C

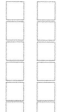

TEST YOURSELF

UNITS 1 & 2

VOCABULARY

1 **Complete the sentences with the words in the list. There are two extra words.**

signed | wrote | brave | guess | recognise | creative
missed | won | wonder | believe | realise | active

1 It was my first competition, and I _____ it!
2 My granddad's quite old, but he's still very _____ – he's always doing things!
3 When his daughter was born, he _____ a song about her.
4 I didn't like the birthday cards in the shop, so I decided to be _____ and make one.
5 It's strange that Maggie isn't here. I _____ where she is.
6 It's eleven o'clock! Wow! I didn't _____ it was so late.
7 I didn't know the answer, so I had to _____ .
8 She didn't run away when the dog was running towards her – she was very _____ .
9 I'm sure he saw me, but he didn't say hello. Maybe he didn't _____ me.
10 I enjoyed my year in the USA, but I really _____ my family.

/10

GRAMMAR

2 **Complete the sentences with the words in the list. You need to write the correct form of the verbs.**

not see (x2) | not open (x2) | bus | the bus

1 My parents gave me my present this morning, but I _____ it yet.
2 I'm tired, I don't want to walk. Let's go by _____ .
3 She was at the party? Really? I _____ her there.
4 There was a sign on the door that said 'No entry!', so I _____ it.
5 There's a new film at the cinema, but I _____ it yet.
6 We were late because _____ arrived 30 minutes late.

3 **Find and correct the mistake in each sentence.**

1 Can I have a glass of a water, please?
2 I've travelled to already more than ten countries.
3 We've lived here since three years.
4 I've gone to a party last night.
5 This is my bicycle. I had it for two years.
6 It's important to eat a lot of the fruit if you want to be healthy.

/12

FUNCTIONAL LANGUAGE

4 **Write the missing words. Choose from the words in the list.**

afraid | Can | definitely | go | idea | Let's | OK | thinking

1 A _____ I use your dictionary, please?
  B Sorry, I'm _____ I'm using it right now.
2 A _____ watch a film on DVD tonight.
  B That's a great _____ !
3 A I'm _____ about doing a walk for charity. What do you think?
  B Yes, you should _____ do it.
4 A Is it _____ if I use your computer?
  B Yes, of course, _____ ahead.

/8

MY SCORE **/30**

| 22 – 30 |
| 10 – 21 |
| 0 – 9 |

29

READING

1 Match the words and pictures. Write 1–6 in the boxes.

1 a video game | 2 a concert | 3 a film
4 a play | 5 a sports event | 6 a TV programme

2 SPEAKING Which of these kinds of entertainment do you like? Tell your partner.

3 SPEAKING Work in small groups. Talk about the things in Exercise 1. Say why people like or don't like them. Use the words in the list to help you.

relaxing | interesting | fun | expensive
crowds | friends | enjoyable

> *I think people enjoy watching a film because it is relaxing.*

4 Look at the pictures and the title of the article on the next page. What do you think the article is about?

1 the high price of horror films
2 the salaries of famous film actors
3 a film that was made very cheaply

5 ◄)) 1.21 Read and listen to the article and check your ideas.

6 Read the article again. Find:

1 two examples of very expensive films.
2 two reasons why it is possible to say that *Monsters* was successful.
3 four reasons why *Monsters* wasn't expensive to make.
4 the amount of time Gareth Edwards worked on the film after filming.

A

B

C

D

E

F

Big movies
on a small budget ■ ■ ■ ■ ■

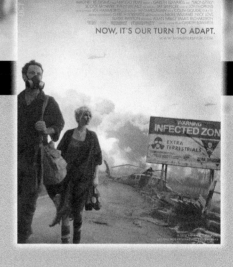

Do you need millions of dollars to make a movie? No. Do you need millions of dollars to make a *successful* movie? Most people would answer 'Yes' to that question. But would they be right?

We're used to hearing about really expensive Hollywood films. The 1997 Oscar-winner *Titanic* cost $200 million to make, and more recently, *Spider Man 3*, one of the most successful films of 2007, had a budget of more than $250 million.

To be successful, however, a film doesn't need to be as expensive as the big Hollywood blockbusters. An example of this is the 2010 movie *Monsters*, which cost less than half a million dollars to make. *Monsters* is set in Mexico and is the story of two people trying to escape from aliens and get back to the USA. The film won several awards and got very good reviews from many film critics – for example, the website Moviefone put *Monsters* at number 3 in its list of the best sci-fi films for 2010.

How did they make the film so cheaply? First of all, it only took three weeks to film, and the film crew was just seven people in a van. Secondly, the man who made the film, Gareth Edwards, decided to film it with digital video,

which is cheaper than the usual 35mm film. (The film equipment cost only $15,000 altogether.) There is also the fact that they used real locations, not a studio. And the cast of the film were Edwards himself and two friends of his – all the extras in the film were people who were just there, and they weren't paid.

Most importantly, Edwards did most of the production work himself. He spent eight months editing *Monsters* and then five months creating the special effects. And he did it all at home on his computer, using non-professional software. The amazing thing is that the final film looks nearly as professional as big, fancy Hollywood productions.

Not everybody liked *Monsters*, of course. One person said: 'That's 90 minutes of my life that I'll never get back.' But overall, it was very well received. And at least it wasn't expensive to make.

■ THiNK VALUES ■

Spending wisely

1 **Read the sentences. How much do you agree with each one? Write a number: 1 (I agree) or 2 (I'm not sure) or 3 (I don't agree).**

   1 If something is expensive, you can be sure it's really good. ☐
   2 Expensive things are usually not worth the money. ☐
   3 You can find really good things that don't cost a lot of money. ☐
   4 It doesn't matter how much something costs. ☐
   5 It's crazy to like something just because it is expensive. ☐

2 **Compare your ideas in the class.**

> *I don't agree with number one. Some expensive things aren't good.*

> *Do you think so? I agree with it. If you buy cheap things, they're usually not good.*

GRAMMAR
Comparative and superlative adjectives (review)

1 Complete these sentences about the article on page 31 with the correct form of the words in the list. Then complete the rules.

good | cheap | boring | expensive

1 They used digital video because it's _____ than 35mm film.

2 Moviefone thought *Monsters* was one of the _____ films of the year.

3 Most Hollywood films are _____ than *Monsters*.

4 One person thought *Monsters* was the _____ film ever.

(not) as … as comparatives

2 Look at the examples of (*not*) *as … as* to compare things. Answer the questions. Then complete the rule.

Extras aren't as expensive as actors.
Monsters looks as professional as Hollywood films.

1 Who are more expensive: extras or actors?

2 Do Hollywood films look more professional than *Monsters*?

RULE: When we want to say that two things are (not) the same, we can use (*not*) _____ + adjective + _____ .

3 Complete each sentence with ideas of your own.

1 Football isn't as exciting as *skiing* .

2 Football is more exciting than *golf* .

3 Potatoes are healthier than _____ .

4 Potatoes aren't as healthy as _____ .

5 English is easier than _____ .

6 English isn't as easy as _____ .

7 Watching TV isn't as good as _____ .

8 Watching TV is better than _____ .

4 Complete the second sentence so it has the same meaning as the first. Use the word in brackets.

0 Ben's sister is younger than him. (old)
Ben's sister *isn't as old as* him.

1 Travelling by train is faster than travelling by bus. (slow)
Travelling by train _____ travelling by bus.

2 Tom is 1.65. Sue is 1.65, too. (tall)
Tom _____ Sue.

3 Dogs are noisier than cats. (quiet)
Dogs _____ cats.

4 This mobile phone costs €225. And the bicycle costs €225, too. (expensive)
The mobile phone _____ the bicycle.

5 Jo thinks geography is easier than history. (difficult)
Jo thinks geography _____ history.

6 My room is tidier than yours. (untidy)
My room _____ yours.

Pronunciation
Words ending in /ə/
Go to page 120. 🔊

Workbook page 28

VOCABULARY
Types of films

Workbook page 31

1 Write the types of films in the list under the pictures.

action film | animated film | documentary comedy | horror film | romantic comedy (rom com) science fiction (sci-fi) | thriller

2 SPEAKING Can you think of an example of each kind of film? Are there any films which are more than one kind?

Madagascar is an animated film and it's a comedy, too.

 1 _____

 2 _____

 3 _____

 4 _____

 5 _____

 6 _____

 7 _____

 8 _____

LISTENING

1 🔊 1.24 **Listen to Part 1 of an interview. Why is Sandra Allen a guest on the radio show?**

1 She won a prize for acting.
2 She won a prize for making a film.
3 She made a film and hopes to win a prize.

2 🔊 1.25 **Listen to Part 2 of the interview.**
✱ **Choose the correct answers.**

1 She chose one of the actors for her film because
  A he wanted to act at school.
  B he had useful things for making the film.
  C he was in the football team.

2 When she wrote the script for the film, Sandra
  A tried to make it shorter.
  B included a lot of different people and places.
  C asked a friend to improve it.

3 Sandra says that the most important thing for making a film is
  A having special equipment.
  B seeing the final film in your head.
  C editing the film to make it shorter.

3 🔊 1.26 **Listen to Part 3, in which Sandra says what her film is about. Complete the text.**

It starts in a school classroom – I used my school of course, and ¹_____ sitting around. And the two actors are sitting talking ²_____ and they start saying how everything is really boring, you know? And another guy is watching them and ³_____, and then he gets up and walks down a corridor into ⁴_____ . And in there, we see him pull a big, black handle – and everything goes into ⁵_____ ! And everyone at the school is surprised and ⁶_____ but they don't know what's happened. So the film is about how everyone really, really wants to get the colour ⁷_____ . In the end, everything does go ⁸_____ . And the couple in the film are in the same place, but now they see it ⁹_____ .

GRAMMAR

Making a comparison stronger or weaker

1 **Read the sentences. Circle the phrase that has a different meaning from the other two. Then complete the rules.**

0 I think independent movies are *a lot / much /* (*a little*) more interesting.
1 I had to make it *a little / a lot / a bit* shorter.
2 The final script was *a little / much / far* better than the first version.

> **RULE:** Use _____ / _____ / *far* to make a comparative stronger.
> Use *a bit* / _____ to make a comparative weaker.

2 **Rewrite these sentences using the words in brackets.**

0 Snakes are more dangerous than bears. (a lot)
  Snakes are a lot more dangerous than bears.
1 My brother is taller than me. (a bit)
2 My new phone's better than the old one. (far)
3 Her nails are longer than yours. (a little)
4 The film's more exciting than the book. (much)

3 **Write sentences comparing these things. Use *much / far / a lot*, or *a bit / a little*.**

1 watching TV / reading a book (interesting / easy)
  I think watching TV is a lot more interesting than reading a book – and it's far easier, too.
2 a mobile phone / an MP4 player (useful / expensive)
3 gorillas / snakes (dangerous / beautiful)
4 English / Art (difficult / interesting)
5 my country / USA (big / beautiful)

Workbook page 29 ➜

THiNK SELF-ESTEEM

The film of my life

1 **Write some ideas for a film script based on your life. Think about these things as you write.**

1 How old are you at the beginning of the film?
2 Which other people will be in the film with you?
3 What will be the funniest scene in the film?
4 How will you end the film?

2 SPEAKING **Work in pairs. Talk about your films.**

READING

1 Read the TV listings. Write the type of programme on each channel.

CHANNEL 1	CHANNEL 2	CHANNEL 3	CHANNEL 4	CHANNEL 5
8.00 pm **Down Our Street**	**8.00 pm** **Double Your Money**	**8.00 pm** **19th-century House**	**8.00 pm** **The News**	**8.00 pm** **The Jordan Baker Show**
Your favourite soap continues with Jim and Amanda having an argument, while Alex still can't find a job. Tom has asked Joanna to marry him but she's got some doubts, and then her friend Tracey tells her a few things about Tom that she didn't know!	Jason Oates is the host of the popular game show where the contestants can win £10,000 – and then double it! There are questions on all kinds of topics to test everyone's general knowledge. Which of tonight's players will get the chance to double their money?	Our reality show continues, now with only eight of the twelve contestants, all living in a house from 200 years ago. It isn't easy living with no electricity, no heating and no 21st-century technology at all. And it's even more difficult with cameras on you 24 hours a day. (Don't forget to have your phone ready to vote.)	All the news and sport from around the world. With Michael Webster.	Jordan Baker presents her completely new chat show. She talks to great celebrity guests and asks them the questions that everyone wants to know the answers to. Tonight, athletics star Sally Malone.
soap opera				

2 Read the programme descriptions again. Answer the questions.

1 Which two programmes have contestants?
2 Which three programmes have presenters?
3 Which programme has actors in it?
4 Which programme asks viewers to participate?

3 **PET** Read these tweets. Match the tweets with the programmes.

Adam Windsor @adamgwindsor   4m
They were really bad this week. I answered all the questions easily. I did better than them! All that money and nobody won it! #DYM

Jenny Kool @kooljenny   15m
Ha ha She needs to think carefully before she says Yes. More carefully than her sister before she got married. Reckon she should say No! lol
#joannathinkaboutit

Paul @earlybird2015   17m
Can't understand what Gavin says when he speaks. He should speak more clearly. Going to vote him off. Hope Jackie wins lol!
#gojackiego

4 **SPEAKING** Work in groups. Choose one of the programmes to watch tonight. Tell the others why you chose it.

> I'm going to watch *Double Your Money* because I really like quiz shows. You can learn things, and it's fun to watch the contestants — especially when they get the answers wrong!

GRAMMAR
Adverbs and comparative adverbs

1 Look at the sentences from the TV listings. Complete them with the words in the list.

popular | easy | easily | carefully

1 It isn't _____ living without electricity.
2 I answered the questions _____ .
3 She needs to think _____ .
4 He's the host of a _____ game show.

2 Circle the adverbs in the previous exercise. Then complete the rules with *adjective* and *adverb*.

> **RULES:**
>
> - Use an _____ to talk about a noun:
>   He's a **slow runner**.
> - Use an _____ to talk about a verb:
>   He **runs slowly**.
>
> We usually form an _____ by adding *-ly*
> (or *-ily*) to the _____ , but some adverbs are
> irregular: *fast → fast, good → well*.

3 Write the adverbs.

0	quick	*quickly*	4	good	_____
1	careful	_____	5	bad	_____
2	clever	_____	6	easy	_____
3	clear	_____	7	fast	_____

4 Look at the examples of comparative adverbs from the tweets on page 34. Then complete the rules.

1 She should think **more carefully** than her sister did.

2 He should speak **more clearly**.

3 I answered the questions **better** than them.

> **RULE:** To form the comparative of most regular adverbs, add the word _____ before the adverb.
>
> If an adverb has one syllable, make the comparative by adding *-er*: *soon → sooner, hard → harder, fast → faster*.
>
> - There are some irregular comparative adverbs: *badly → worse, well → better*.
> - Notice that the comparative of *early* is written *earlier*.

5 Complete the sentences. Use the comparative adverb forms of the words in brackets.

0 Sue runs _*faster*_ (fast) than me.

1 Graham writes _____ (clear) than me.

2 You need to do your homework _____ (careful) if you want to get good marks.

3 Sorry, I don't understand. Can you speak _____ (slow), please?

4 The party starts at ten o'clock, but you can come _____ (early) if you want to.

5 I only got 22% in the test, but you did even _____ (bad) than me!

6 Sandra always works _____ (hard) than the other kids.

7 Martina speaks English _____ (good) than I do.

Workbook page 29

VOCABULARY
Types of TV programmes

1 Look at the different types of TV programmes. Can you think of an example for each one?

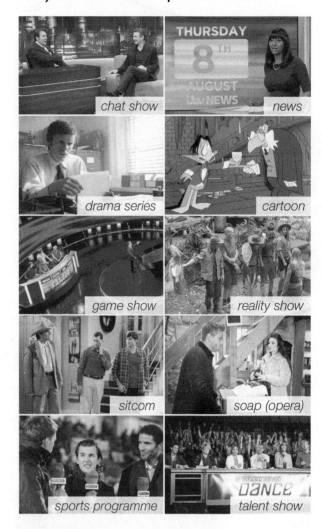

chat show — news

drama series — cartoon

game show — reality show

sitcom — soap (opera)

sports programme — talent show

2 **SPEAKING** Work in pairs. Ask and answer the questions.

1 What kind(s) of programmes do you really like?

2 What kind(s) of programmes do you really NOT like?

3 What programme on TV now do you always watch? Why?

4 What programme on TV now do you never watch? Why?

5 How do you watch TV programmes – on TV, on your phone, on a tablet …?

Workbook page 31

WRITING
A paragraph

Write a paragraph about your TV habits.

- Use your answers to the questions in Vocabulary Exercise 2 to help you.

- Try to use grammar and vocabulary from the unit (comparative adjectives, words for TV programmes, etc.)

Extras

1 **Look at the photos and answer the questions.**

Why does Megan want to be an extra in the film?
Why is Megan unhappy in the last photo?

2 🔊 1.27 **Now read and listen to the photostory. Check your answers.**

LUKE Guys, guys! Guess what!
OLIVIA They're going to make a film here.
LUKE Oh. Right. You've heard then?
RYAN We have. They're going to do some filming in the park. For a new sci-fi movie. And Megan's really excited.
MEGAN I really am. Gregory Harris is in the film. He's so cool. In fact, I think he's my favourite actor of all time!

1

LUKE Don't get too excited, Megan. You're not going to meet him. Or even see him, probably.
RYAN Don't be so sure, Luke. The thing is, they want extras for the film.
LUKE Extras?
MEGAN You know – the people who stand around and do things but don't say anything.
LUKE Oh, come on, Megan. Everybody knows what extras are.

2

MEGAN Oh, sorry. Anyway, they're going to choose people to be extras today. One o'clock at the Sports Centre in town. I'm definitely going. Imagine – me, in a film with Gregory Harris!
OLIVIA Ryan's going, and so am I. How about you, Luke?
LUKE OK, why not? One o'clock at the Sports Centre? Let's all meet there then.

3

RYAN That's odd. There's no one here.
OLIVIA Have a look at this, guys. The time was eleven o'clock, not one o'clock.
MEGAN Oh, no! I read it wrong. I saw eleven and thought it was one! Oh, how could I be so stupid?
LUKE Looks like you're not going to meet Gregory Harris after all, Megan.
MEGAN Oh, leave me alone, Luke!

4

DEVELOPING SPEAKING

3 Work in pairs. Discuss what happens next in the story. Write down your ideas.

We think Ryan goes to see the film director to try to help Megan.

4 ▶ EP2 Watch to find out how the story continues.

5 Mark the sentences T (true) or F (false).

1 Tony Gorman is from Britain. ___
2 He is the director of the film. ___
3 He buys a coffee for Megan. ___
4 Megan listens to Tony's phone call. ___
5 Megan recognises the second man who comes into the coffee shop. ___
6 She comes back to the park with an autographed photo of Gregory Harris. ___

PHRASES FOR FLUENCY

1 Find the expressions 1–6 in the story. Who says them? How do you say them in your language?

1 Guess what?   4 Have a look [at this]
2 In fact, …   5 Looks like …
3 Come on, …   6 … after all.

2 Complete the conversation. Use the expressions in Exercise 1.

JIM   Hi guys. ¹_____ ? I'm in the football team!
MIKE   You're joking!
JIM   No, I'm not. ²_____ at this. It's the team list.
MIKE   But you're not a good player, Jim. ³_____ , you're terrible!
ALICE Oh, ⁴_____ , Mike! He's not so bad.
SUSIE That's right. And the school has picked him to play, so ⁵_____ you're wrong, Mike.
MIKE   Well, I guess so.
JIM   Yes. I'm good enough for the school team ⁶_____ !

WordWise
Expressions with *get*

1 Look at the sentences from the unit so far. Choose the correct meaning of *get* in each one.

1 They're trying to **get** back to the USA.
2 Can I **get** you another drink?
3 Who will **get** the chance to double their money?
4 Don't **get** too excited, Megan.

a become   c go, arrive
b receive   d bring, buy

2 Use a phrase from the list to complete each sentence.

get home | got bored | got there
get a drink | get angry | got better

1 The film was terrible – after 20 minutes, I _____ and fell asleep.
2 I was really late for school – when I _____ , it was already ten o'clock!
3 There's still a long way to go. We won't _____ before midnight, I think.
4 He was ill for about a week, but then he _____ , I'm happy to say.
5 It was just a joke. Please don't _____ with me!
6 If you want, we can _____ in that café in the town centre.

3 Match the questions and answers.

1 Let's go and get a drink. ☐
2 When do you get angry with people? ☐
3 Do you ever get bored watching TV? ☐
4 What time do you get to school? ☐
5 Do you ever get a cold? ☐

a When they say things I don't like.
b Usually about eight o'clock.
c OK. The shop over there sells water.
d Sometimes – in winter, usually.
e Only when it's a programme I don't like.

4 Now write *your* answers to questions 2–5 in Exercise 3.

Workbook page 31 ▶

FUNCTIONS
Asking for and offering help

1 Look at two sentences from the video. Which one is asking for help? Which one is offering help?

1 Can I help you?
2 Could you help me with something?

2 Now look at these sentences. Are they asking or offering help?

1 Can you lend me a hand?
2 Do you need any help?
3 Have you got a few minutes?
4 Is everything OK?

3 SPEAKING Work in pairs. Use the questions in Exercises 1 and 2 to act out conversations in a shop, at home, at school and other places.

4 SOCIAL NETWORKING

OBJECTIVES

FUNCTIONS: giving advice
GRAMMAR: indefinite pronouns
(everyone, no one, someone, etc.)
all / some / none / any of them;
should(n't), had better, ought to
VOCABULARY: IT terms; language
for giving advice

READING

1 SPEAKING Work in pairs. Answer the questions.

1 Which of these social networks do you know about?
2 What do you think of them?
3 Do you know about any other social networks?

2 SPEAKING Read these statements about using social networks. Which of them are true for you? Discuss them with a partner.

1 I've got a Facebook account but hardly ever use it.
2 I don't post many comments, but I like to read other people's posts.
3 I constantly check for updates on social media.
4 I sometimes post comments that I regret later.
5 I know of a post that created a problem.

3 ◀))1.28 Read and listen to the article about online behaviour to decide if each sentence is correct or incorrect. If it's correct, mark it A. If it's incorrect, mark it B.

1 James Miller did not think before he wrote a post and so he lost his job. ☐
2 His boss apologised for giving James work that wasn't very interesting. ☐
3 Cathy's birthday party ended in disaster because her parents went out that evening. ☐
4 A study from last year shows a lot of teens had problems because of their behaviour on the web. ☐
5 The writer of the article thinks that you can't make everybody happy with your posts. ☐
6 He says that before writing a post you should think of reactions you might get. ☐
7 He thinks that we need to be as friendly online as we are in real life. ☐
8 He says that posting things when you're unhappy is a good way to feel better. ☐

4 Work in pairs. Correct the statements marked B.

Think before you act online

Sometimes what we post on our favourite social networks can have consequences we didn't expect. One weekend, 20-year-old James Miller posted on his Facebook page that his job was 'soooo boring'. When he got to work on Monday his boss told him to clear his desk and get out. He gave him a letter, too. It said: 'After reading your comments on Facebook about our company, we understand you are not happy with your work. We think it is better for you to look for something that you will find more interesting.'

A few years ago, a girl's birthday party turned into a nightmare. Fifteen-year-old Cathy posted an invitation to her birthday party online. She posted her address, too. When her parents got back from the cinema that evening, they couldn't believe their eyes. There were 500 people at the party, and some of them were smashing windows, breaking potted plants and making a total mess of the house.

Most teens think they know everything about social media, and that things like this could never happen to them. A study shows that last year alone, more than three million young people worldwide got into trouble because of their online activities.

Here are some important tips. None of them can guarantee 100% Internet security, but all of them will help you to be safer online.

RULE 1: Share with care!

Not everyone will like what you write on Facebook or Twitter. Think before you post something. You can never completely control who sees your profile, your texts, your pictures, or your videos. Before clicking 'post', everyone should ask themselves two questions: 'How will I feel if my family or teachers see this?' and 'How might this post be bad for me in three, five or ten years from now?'

RULE 2: Be polite when you write!

Imagine someone is unfriendly in real life. You don't like it, right? Well, the same is true of online communication. Politeness matters, and anyone can be polite. No one likes it when you 'shout' in your messages. DON'T USE ALL CAPITALS!!!!!!!! If you feel angry or frustrated while you're writing a message, wait a bit. Read it again later and then send it.

RULE 3: Protect and respect!

Don't share your passwords with anyone. Don't post your home or email address online. Beware of 'cyberbullying' – don't forward rumours about other people, and don't say negative things about them. If you get messages like that or see them online, talk to an adult you know.

■ THiNK VALUES ■

Responsible online behaviour

1 Read the statements. Write them in two lists under *Do* and *Don't*.

- say bad things about other people online.
- talk to your teacher or another adult if you get bullied on social media.
- think carefully before you write a post about yourself or other people.
- write a post about someone when you are angry with them.
- write posts containing personal information about your family.
- think before you post a photo of yourself or someone else.

2 SPEAKING Work in pairs. Compare your lists with your partner. Think of at least two more statements for each list.

GRAMMAR
Indefinite pronouns (*everyone*, *no one*, *someone* etc.)

1 Complete these sentences from the article on page 39. Underline other examples of indefinite pronouns in the article.

1 Most teens think they know _____ about social media.

2 Think before you post _____ .

3 _____ likes it when you 'shout' in your messages.

2 Complete the table. Use the article on page 39 to help you. Then complete the rule with *some / any / no / every*.

everything	something	nothing	anything
everyone	1 _____	2 _____	3 _____
everywhere	somewhere	nowhere	anywhere

> **RULE:** The words beginning with
> - _____ mean 'all' (people / things / places).
> - _____ mean that we don't know exactly which (person / thing / place).
> - _____ mean that we don't care or it doesn't matter which (person / thing / place).
> - _____ mean 'not any' (person / thing / place).

3 Complete the sentences with words from the table in Exercise 2.

1 Where's my pen? I've looked _____ , but I can't find it.

2 Using social media can be a real problem. _____ should know that.

3 The teacher asked a question, but _____ knew the answer.

4 _____ left a message for you at reception.

5 Ouch! There's _____ in my eye!

6 I've no idea where Sally is. She could be _____ .

7 Do you want a place to relax on your holiday? There's _____ better than here!

8 It's so noisy. Let's go _____ quieter.

4 Complete the sentences so that they are true for you.

1 Everyone knows that I …

2 For my next holiday I'd like to go somewhere …

3 I don't like eating anything that has got … in it.

4 I think anyone can learn to …

Workbook page 36

VOCABULARY
IT terms

1 Match the phrases with the definitions. Write the numbers 1–10.

1 to key in your password
2 to install a programme
3 to attach a file | 4 to have network coverage
5 to upload a photo | 6 to delete a message
7 ~~to open an attachment~~ | 8 to buy an app
9 to activate flight mode
10 to download a file

a to click on the icon of a file that comes with an email `7`

b to have a signal that lets you make phone calls, etc. ☐

c to add a separate element (e.g. a photo, a document, a video) to an email ☐

d to make an image available on the Internet ☐

e to pay for a programme for your mobile or tablet ☐

f to type a secret word that gives you access to a computer ☐

g to put a programme on a computer ☐

h to switch on a function on your mobile or tablet so you can't go online ☐

i to remove a piece of text so it cannot be seen any more ☐

j to copy information or a programme from the Internet onto your computer hard disk ☐

2 **SPEAKING** Work in pairs. Ask and answer the questions.

1 How easy or difficult is it for you to go online?

2 How often do you post something on social media?

3 What kind of things do you usually post?

4 What ways do you know of keeping passwords secure but remembering them?

3 Draw mind maps for these verbs.

Workbook page 38

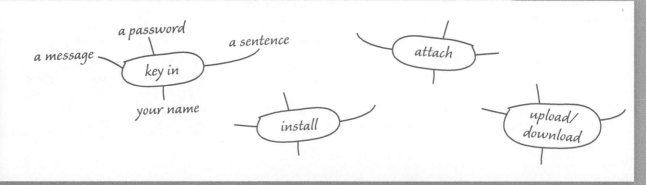

LISTENING

1 Match the phrases with the definitions. Write the numbers 1–6.

1 you get an error message | **2** an application closes down | **3** your screen goes blank | **4** you close a file without saving it first | **5** a programme freezes **6** your hard disk crashes

a your computer monitor does not show any information any more ☐

b a programme shuts down ☐

c you lose all the changes you've just made ☐

d information appears on your computer screen telling you about a problem ☐

e the system that saves information on your computer suddenly stops working ☐

f an application stops working, and the screen will not change no matter what you do ☐

2 SPEAKING Work in pairs. Answer the questions.

1 Which of the problems in Exercise 1 have you experienced?

2 How do you usually solve computer problems?

3 ◀)) 1.29 Listen to Hannah and her dad. Answer these questions.

1 What's Hannah's dad trying to do?

2 What mistake has he made?

4 ◀)) 1.29 Listen again. Look at the six sentences.
✳ Decide if each sentence is correct or incorrect. If it is correct, put a tick (✓) under A. If it is not correct, put a tick under B.

		A	B
1	Hannah's dad likes gaming a lot.		
2	He's not happy when Hannah's brother spends his time playing computer games.		
3	Hannah says she'll tell her brother about their dad's interest in gaming.		
4	Dad didn't know that he had to create his own username and password.		
5	When Hannah tells him to choose a team, he's not very patient.		
6	Hannah reads out an error message that appears on the screen.		

GRAMMAR
all / some / none / any of them

1 Complete the sentence. Look back at the article on page 39 to check.

There were 500 people at the party, and
⁰ _some of them_ were smashing windows and breaking potted plants.
Here are some important tips – ¹_____ can guarantee 100% internet security, but
²_____ will help you to be safer online.

2 Complete the rule with *things / more / none*.

> **RULE:** We use the expressions *all / some / _____ / any of them* to refer back to a group (of _____ or people) and say _____ about it.

3 Choose the correct words.

1 My friends had a great time at my birthday party. *All / None* of them wanted to leave!

2 I have no idea which of these pens is Carla's. They all look exactly the same, so *any / some* of them could be hers.

3 These bikes all look good, but I'm sure *some / any* of them are better than others.

4 These T-shirts are really cool. *None / Any* of them would be fine for me.

5 These caps weren't expensive. I got *all / none* of them for £12.

6 We tried lots of different jeans, but *none / some* of them were the right size for me.

7 All the questions were really hard – I couldn't answer *none / any* of them!

8 Her songs are OK – I quite like *some / any* of them.

4 Complete the sentences with *all / some / none / any*. (There may be more than one possible answer.)

1 There are 32 students in Sarah's class. It's amazing that ___*all*___ of them like music, but _____ of them listen to jazz.

2 I like most American TV shows, but _____ of them are terrible!

3 OK, he scored three goals – but _____ of them were lucky!

4 The cakes that I made were horrible – we couldn't eat _____ of them, so we threw them all away.

5 My three brothers like IT, but _____ of them is as good with computers as my sister.

6 Look at those cameras. _____ of them are very cheap, but others are very expensive.

> Workbook page 36

READING

1 Look at the mixed-up messages. Match them with the types of communication in the list. Write letters a–f.

1 text message ☐   4 online post ☐
2 text message ☐   5 email ☐
3 notice ☐   6 note ☐

2 Read the messages. Mark the correct answer A, B or C.

1 What should Emily's mum do?
   A Tell Benjamin to do the shopping for the family.
   B Warm up some food and buy a birthday present.
   C Make sure Benjamin knows Emily will be late.

2 What's the purpose of Benjamin's note?
   A To inform Emily of what Lucas said
   B To find out why Lucas phoned
   C To borrow a bike from Lucas

3 On her Facebook page, Emily
   A has posted photos of their trip.
   B asks Lucas what he thinks of the photos.
   C wants to say that she didn't like the trip.

4 The advert says the mountain bike
   A is almost new and in good condition.
   B is not the right bike for girls.
   C is in excellent condition, but expensive.

5 What should Lucas do?
   A Lower the price.
   B Give Emily a call.
   C Buy Emily a ring.

6 Lucas writes a text message
   A to invite Emily to join him again on Sunday.
   B to tell Emily that the weather is not good.
   C to invite his friends on a bike ride.

■TRAIN TO THINK■

Logical sequencing

1 Read the messages again. Work out a logical order. Write letters a–f in the right order.

☐ 1   ☐ 3   ☐ 5
☐ 2   ☐ 4   ☐ 6

2 SPEAKING Work in pairs. Compare your ideas with a partner. Discuss any differences.

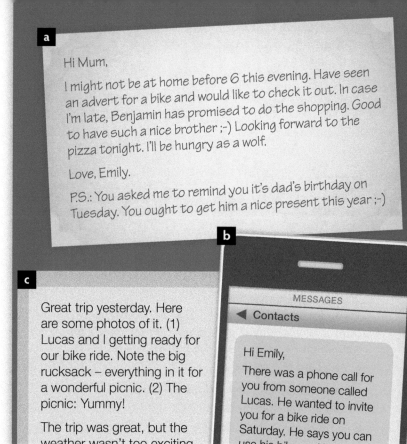

a

Hi Mum,

I might not be at home before 6 this evening. Have seen an advert for a bike and would like to check it out. In case I'm late, Benjamin has promised to do the shopping. Good to have such a nice brother ;-) Looking forward to the pizza tonight. I'll be hungry as a wolf.

Love, Emily.

P.S.: You asked me to remind you it's dad's birthday on Tuesday. You ought to get him a nice present this year ;-)

b

MESSAGES
◀ Contacts

Hi Emily,

There was a phone call for you from someone called Lucas. He wanted to invite you for a bike ride on Saturday. He says you can use his bike and he'll borrow a friend's.

Oh, la la!

Benji

c

Great trip yesterday. Here are some photos of it. (1) Lucas and I getting ready for our bike ride. Note the big rucksack – everything in it for a wonderful picnic. (2) The picnic: Yummy!

The trip was great, but the weather wasn't too exciting. Pity we didn't get to the top. Had to turn back – fog and rain.

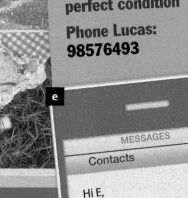

d

FOR SALE
Mountain bike, bought last month, used 3 times – perfect condition
Phone Lucas:
98576493

e

MESSAGES
Contacts

Hi E,

Best Saturday for a long time. I never knew rain and fog can be so much fun.

I'd like to try again next Sunday. You'd better join me if you don't want to break your promise ;-)!

L

P.S.: Love the photos on Facebook

f

▶ C ⌂

From: Emily
To: Lucas
Hi,
Have thought about it carefully. It's a cool bike, but £400 is a lot more than what I wanted to spend. Sorry!
Anyway, really nice to have met you. What you said about your bike tours sounded lovely. You should give me a ring some time if you want to ;-)
My phone: 97326797.

E

GRAMMAR
Should(n't), had better, ought to

1 **Complete these sentences from the messages on page 42. Then choose the correct words to complete the rule.**

1 You _____ get him a nice present this year!

2 You _____ give me a ring some time if you want to.

3 You _____ join me if you don't want to break your promise.

> **RULE:** *Should, had better* and *ought to* are used to give [1]*advice / information*.
>
> • *Should* and *ought to* mean more or less the same, but we usually don't use *ought to* in questions and negative statements.
>
> • The meaning of *had better* is often a little stronger. The speaker wants to say that there are [2]*positive / negative* consequences if you ignore the advice.
>
> These verbs [3]*do / don't* use an auxiliary verb in the negative: *shouldn't, oughtn't to, had better not*.

2 **Read the questions 1–6. Then match them to the correct answers a–f. Circle the correct word in each answer.**

1 I've broken my friend's MP3 player. What should I do? ☐

2 I've got toothache. What should I do? ☐

3 I didn't do the test very well. What should I do? ☐

4 I'd like to go climbing, but I've never done it before. What should I do? ☐

5 I'm hungry. Should I eat some chocolate? ☐

6 I'm angry with my brother. He said something I didn't like. What should I do? ☐

7 This sweater my sister gave me looks terrible. I don't like it at all. What should I do? ☐

a You *should / shouldn't* eat it. Fruit is healthier.

b You *should / shouldn't* tell him. It's best to be honest with him.

c You'd *better / better not* return it to the shop. That would really hurt her feelings.

d You *shouldn't / ought to* go back and study everything again.

e You'd *better / shouldn't* get some training. It can be dangerous.

f You *ought to / shouldn't* see a dentist.

g You'd *better / shouldn't* say sorry the next time you meet your friend.

3 **Look at these pictures. Write short dialogues with (serious or funny) answers giving advice.**

1 *Boy* What should I do?
 Girl You should throw a sausage over the fence so the dog won't attack you.

Workbook page 37

VOCABULARY
Language for giving advice

1 **Look at the words and phrases below and answer the questions.**

bad / good / practical / useful advice
advice about [something]
to take / follow [someone's] advice
to ignore [someone's] advice
to advise [someone] [to do something]
to advise against [something]
advisable

a What's the difference between *advice* and *advise*?

b Which of the phrases mean(s)
 – not to listen to somebody's advice?
 – do what somebody has advised you to do?

c How do you say 'advisable' in your language?

2 **Complete the sentences with phrases from Exercise 1. Use the correct verb forms.**

1 I've told Peter he shouldn't post photos like that, but he has always _____ my _____ .

2 Should I buy a tablet or a laptop? Can you give me some _____ what's better?

3 He wants to become a web designer. His dad has _____ him to take a course. He should _____ that _____ .

4 My uncle has a heart problem. This web page _____ fatty foods.

Workbook page 38

FUNCTIONS
Giving advice

SPEAKING **Ask and answer questions with a partner.**

1 Imagine you meet somebody who has never used a computer. What advice would you give them about social networking?

2 Are you good at giving advice? Say why (not) and give examples.

3 When do you find it difficult to follow someone's advice?

Culture

1 Look at the photos. What do they show?

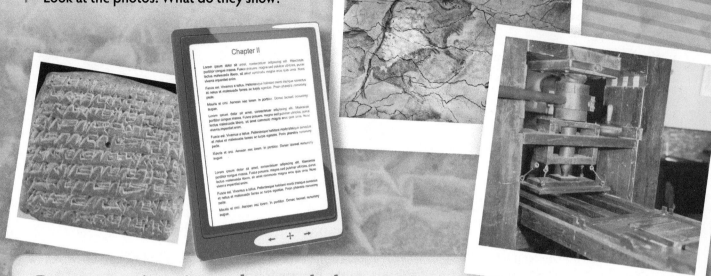

Communication through history

1 ☐

Cave paintings are the oldest pictures. Some of them, for example the beautiful images in the caves of Altamira in the north of Spain, are almost 30,000 years old. Many of these paintings show animals or hunting scenes. The images do not have written words. But when we look at them, we get an idea of the emotions the people felt when drawing them. The paintings tell stories of hopes and fears. They are an early form of communication.

2 ☐

Sometime between 4000 and 3000 BCE, people in Egypt and Mesopotamia developed the skill of writing. They engraved text on stone tablets first. But it was impossible to carry stones from place to place. The invention of papyrus allowed documents to be moved easily. Writing on papyrus made it easier to correct mistakes too. And do you know how they did that? When a scribe – the person who wrote the documents – made a mistake, they licked the ink off the papyrus before it got dry and made their corrections!

3 ☐

People made the first books from papyrus and from thin animal skins. Paper was invented in China as early as 105 CE. The quality of paper soon became very good. The world's oldest known printed book is from China too. It was published on May 11, 868 CE. In Europe, books were written manually until the middle of the 15th century when Johannes Gutenberg invented the printing press in Germany. Since that time, almost 140 million books have been published worldwide. For many people, one of life's greatest pleasures is spending a few hours in a bookshop browsing through the books.

4 ☐

Books will be around for many years, of course. But some people prefer reading e-books. They are easier to take with you when you travel, and you can download them instantly from the Internet. Now you can buy your books whenever you want without having to leave the comfort of your home.

2 🔊 1.30 Read and listen to the article again. Match the paragraph headings with the paragraphs. Write the letters a–f. Note that there are two headings you don't need.

 a The invention of books by Gutenberg
 b Early forms of written communication
 c Books in their most modern form
 d From stone tablets to the printing press
 e Communication without reading and writing
 f The history of book making

3 SPEAKING Work in pairs. Discuss the questions.

1 How important are books for you? Give reasons.
2 What book(s) have you read recently? How did you like them?
3 Do you prefer books or e-books? Give reasons.

Pronunciation
The short /ʌ/ vowel sound
Go to page 120.

4 VOCABULARY **Read the article again. Find words or phrases with the following meaning.**

0 a large hole underground (paragraph 1) ___cave___
1 happiness, love and anger (paragraph 1) _____
2 cut words into stone (paragraph 2) _____
3 paper made from plants (paragraph 2) _____
4 moved the tongue across something (paragraph 2) _____
5 produced (and sold) a book (paragraph 3) _____
6 a machine to make newspapers, books or magazines (paragraph 3) _____
7 looking through a book or magazine very quickly, without reading everything (paragraph 3) _____

WRITING
A web page giving advice

1 Read this information and decide who it would be important for. Then answer the questions.

1 Where do people use public computers?
2 What other examples not mentioned in the text can you think of?
3 Why should you never save a password on a public computer?
4 What's the problem with just closing the browser when you want to finish a session?

2 Rewrite the sentences by putting the words in brackets in the right position.

1 Read our advice. (carefully)
   Read our advice carefully.
2 Click 'Yes'. (don't)
3 Make you do not simply close the browser. (sure)
4 You should log out. (always)
5 Ask them to go somewhere else. (politely)

3 Are the sentences above used to give advice or to give an opinion? Match each of them with one of the situations below. Write the numbers 1–5.

a when the system asks you 'Do you want to save the password?' ☐
b when you want to leave a site ☐
c to be smart and safe when using public computers ☐
d if someone looks over your shoulder and watches you ☐
e when you finish your session ☐

4 Match the content with the five sections of the text.

Introduction:	a	Don't leave important information on the screen.
Bullet point 1:	b	Log out properly.
Bullet point 2:	c	Don't let people watch you.
Bullet point 3:	d	What is the purpose of this text?
Bullet point 4:	e	Don't save information.

How to use a public computer – safety tips

There are times when you may want to use a public computer, for example in an Internet café, a library or at an airport. That's when it's especially important to be smart and safe.

- Don't save! When you want to log into a social networking website or your web mail, the system will ask you, 'Do you want to save this password?' Don't click 'Yes' when you are working on a public computer.

- Log out! Make sure you do not simply close the browser when you want to leave a site. You should always "log out" of the site when you finish your session.

- Close windows! If you need to walk away from the computer for any reason, you should close all the windows on the computer first. Don't leave any information on the screen that other people shouldn't see.

- Watch out! Be careful about people looking at the screen over your shoulder. Ask them politely to go somewhere else so you can use the computer in private.

5 What would be important advice for good online behaviour? Make notes.

Here are some ideas:
- what (not) to share on social networks
- creating secure passwords and how to keep them safe
- what to do when you receive offensive comments on social websites
- what you should know about uploading photos on social networks

6 Write the text for a web page giving advice on good online behaviour (about 200 words).

- Use an introduction and bullet points to structure your text.
- Use language from Exercises 2 and 3 to give advice, and make sure your readers understand what situations your advice refers to.

▌THiNK EXAMS ▌

READING
Part 2: Matching

Workbook page 42 ➤

1 **These people are looking for a film to watch. Below are six film reviews. Decide which film, A–F, would be most suitable for these people.**

1 Dawn loves thinking about the future. How will life be different? She's a huge fan of films that are set in a time many years from now. But she doesn't really enjoy films that are too frightening.

2 Paula's job is very boring so when she gets home she likes watching a good action film with lots of special effects, but she's not a fan of sci-fi. She also likes films with some exciting bits, too.

3 Keith is a romantic who enjoys a good love story but it must have a happy ending. He doesn't like serious films very much, and likes to have a laugh, too.

4 Lisa is not really a fan of fiction and only watches films about real life. She is interested in anything from history to nature to science as long as she learns something from it.

LISTENING
Part 4: True/false

Workbook page 35 ➤

2 🔊 1.33 **You will hear a conversation between Ellen and her dad. Decide if each sentence is correct or incorrect. If it is correct, put a tick (✓) in the box under A for YES. If it is not correct, put a tick (✓) in the box under B for NO.**

	A YES	B NO
1 Ellen's dad thinks she's been on the computer too long.	☐	☐
2 Ellen's only been on the computer for 30 minutes today.	☐	☐
3 Ellen was looking at a site about Queen Victoria.	☐	☐
4 Ellen's dad wants to see what she's talking to Jenny about.	☐	☐
5 Ellen's dad needs some help baking a cake.	☐	☐
6 Ellen would like to see her dad working in the kitchen.	☐	☐

HOT NEW FILMS ★

A The Invisible World

Using the most advanced camera technology in the world, this documentary takes us to places that have never been filmed before. From deep under the sea to inside the human body, this film contains some of the most amazing images you will ever see.

B The King Who Never Was

In 1936 Edward VIII decided to give up being king after less than a year so he could be with the woman he loved. This film revisits one of the most popular 'royal stories' of all time and mixes fact and fiction to create an interesting drama. It will keep audiences entertained but probably upset many historians.

C It Could Happen to You

Imagine waking up in a house that is not the house you went to sleep in. Imagine not recognising your children – even though they all seem to think you are their mum. This fascinating sci-fi takes us to a future world where people buy and sell memories.

D Will they? Won't they?

Ever since school, Jack and Jill have been best friends. But now they are in their twenties, and their feelings are changing. Is either of them brave enough to see that they are falling in love? Will they do something about it? Of course it is all OK in the end in this likeable but silly rom com.

E Countdown to Disaster

A speeding train is going to crash into a nuclear power station and no one can stop it. Or can they? Special agent Ryan has got an hour to stop the disaster but there's a problem, he has a bomb tied around his waist. Car chases, explosions and amazing special effects – this thriller has got it all.

F Tomorrow Now

The year is 2080 and for the last ten years Earth has been in contact with aliens. Today is the day that we finally welcome them to our planet. How will they change our lives and are they really as friendly as they seem? One of the scariest films you will see this year.

TEST YOURSELF

VOCABULARY

1 **Complete the sentences with the words in the list. There are two extra words.**

comedy | thriller | download | ignore | upload | news
documentary | advice | advise | post | attachment | mode

1 If you're on a plane, you should activate flight _____ on your mobile phone.
2 There was a _____ programme on TV last night – the funniest programme I've ever watched!
3 I've got some great photos here. I'm going to _____ them onto my website tonight.
4 There was an interesting programme last night – a _____ about the history of my country.
5 Let me give you some _____ . Don't go and see that film – it's awful.
6 My father always watches the _____ on TV to see what's happening in the world.
7 I'm sure you think it's a good idea, but I'd _____ against it, to be honest.
8 I'm sending you a photo – it's in the _____ with this email.
9 If you want to talk to me, _____ a message on chat and I'll write back to you.
10 We gave him lots of advice, but he decided to _____ it!

/10

GRAMMAR

2 **Complete the sentences with the words in the list.**

best | better | no one | someone | none | everyone

1 I phoned, but _____ answered.
2 This is the _____ ice cream I've ever tasted.
3 I've got a problem and I need to talk to _____ , please.
4 I asked all my friends, but _____ of them knew the answer.
5 She plays the guitar _____ than me.
6 We had a great time. _____ enjoyed it.

3 **Find and correct the mistake in each sentence.**

1 He's a bit angry – I think you ought apologise to him.
2 The film isn't as good than the book.
3 There are six films on TV, and all of them is terrible!
4 It's the most bad party I've ever been to.
5 He runs more quick than me.
6 It's late. We'd better to go home now.

/12

FUNCTIONAL LANGUAGE

4 **Complete the sentences with the words in the list.**

against | everything | hand | help | ought | should | with | would

1 A Is _____ OK?
  B Yes, thanks. But perhaps I _____ sit down.
2 A Do you need any _____ ?
  B Well, yes, that _____ be great. Thanks!
3 A Could you help me _____ something? I want to borrow some money for a new guitar.
  B Well, you know, I'd advise _____ it. It's really not a good idea.
4 A Joe? This is heavy. Can you lend me a _____ ?
  B Of course, Mum. But you _____ to let me carry the heaviest bags!

/8

MY SCORE /30

| 22 – 30 |
| 10 – 21 |
| 0 – 9 |

OBJECTIVES

FUNCTIONS: asking about feelings; making helpful suggestions

GRAMMAR: present perfect continuous; present perfect simple vs. present perfect continuous

VOCABULARY: making music; musical instruments

1 _____

2 _____

3 _____

4 _____

5 _____

6 _____

READING

1 🔊 1.34 **Listen. What type of music do you hear? Write the words in the pictures.**

rap | jazz | opera | dance music | rock | pop

2 **What other types of music can you think of?**

3 SPEAKING **Work in pairs. What kind of music do you like? Ask and answer questions.**

> Do you like ... ?

> I love/like/can't stand ...

> I've never listened to ...

4 **Look at the photos in the online forum on the next page and answer the questions.**

1 Which picture shows a busker?
2 Which picture shows a talent show?
3 Which of these people do you recognise?
4 Do you know how they became famous?

5 **Read the online forum quickly and check your ideas.**

6 🔊 1.35 **Read and listen to the online forum and answer the questions.**

1 What kind of shows are *The X Factor* and *The Voice*?
2 Who won the first series of *The X Factor*?
3 Where did One Direction finish in 2010's *The X Factor*?
4 What was the first video Justin Bieber's mum put on the Internet?
5 How old was Justin Bieber when Scooter Braun discovered him?
6 How did Lily Allen get tens of thousands of fans?
7 Why is busking good for a new musician?
8 Where did Eric Clapton busk when he was starting out?

Singer songwriter: Any advice?

Hello. I'm a singer songwriter. I'm *good* and I'm going to make it big! Any advice????

Paulie asked 2 days ago Answers (3)

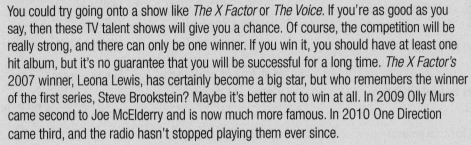

Answer #1 answered 4 hours ago

You could try going onto a show like *The X Factor* or *The Voice*. If you're as good as you say, then these TV talent shows will give you a chance. Of course, the competition will be really strong, and there can only be one winner. If you win it, you should have at least one hit album, but it's no guarantee that you will be successful for a long time. *The X Factor's* 2007 winner, Leona Lewis, has certainly become a big star, but who remembers the winner of the first series, Steve Brookstein? Maybe it's better not to win at all. In 2009 Olly Murs came second to Joe McElderry and is now much more famous. In 2010 One Direction came third, and the radio hasn't stopped playing them ever since.

Answer #2 answered 10 hours ago

Bands have been using the Internet for publicity for years now. It's cheap, quick and easy. Look at Justin Bieber. In 2007, when he was just 12, he entered a local singing competition and came second. His mum filmed him and put it on YouTube. Then she put on some more videos of him singing. In 2008 a talent scout called Scooter Braun accidentally clicked on one of Justin's videos. He really liked what he saw and went to meet the young Bieber. The rest is history. And then there's Lily Allen. She had a contract with a music label, but they were too busy with bigger artists to give her any attention. So she posted some of her music on MySpace. Soon, she had tens of thousands of fans, and lots of attention from her label. Thanks to the Internet, she became a star overnight.

Answer #3 answered 2 days ago

I've been writing songs since I was a teenager. I never really thought about making a record, but when I started my band I also started to get more serious about my music. We haven't been playing together very long, but people say we're really good. Now I'm really keen on making a career in music. I think the best advice is to start small and grow big. We've being doing a lot of busking in the streets and that's helped us get a good local following. We're now getting invitations from clubs in the area to come and play shows. Loads of famous people started out busking. Eric Clapton, one of the greatest guitarists in the world, busked on the streets of London when he was young.

THINK VALUES

Following your dreams

1 **Match these peoples with their dreams.**

1 Jessie is a really good artist. ☐
2 Kylie loves acting. ☐
3 David is great at football. ☐
4 Lance has written a book. ☐

a 'I want to get it published.'
b 'I want to be in a play.'
c 'I want to play professionally.'
d 'I'd love to have an exhibition of my work.'

2 **What should these people do to realise their dreams? Give advice. Make notes for each one.**

David / join club

3 SPEAKING **Work in pairs. Compare your ideas.**

> *David should join a football club. He should practise for three hours every day.*

4 SPEAKING **Discuss these questions in small groups.**

1 What is your dream?
2 What can you do to make it come true?

GRAMMAR
Present perfect continuous

1 **Complete the sentences with the correct form of the words in brackets. Check your answers in the online forum on page 49.**

1 I _____ (write) songs since I was a teenager.

2 We _____ (do) a lot of busking in the streets.

3 We _____ (not play) together very long.

2 **Match the example sentences below with the rules. Write the numbers 1–3.**

1 <u>I've been learning the piano</u> for two years.

2 I've been practising the piano <u>since 10 am.</u>

3 I've been playing the piano all day and <u>I'm tired now.</u>

> **RULE:** The present perfect continuous is used for actions happening over a period of time. We use it to:
>
> **a** emphasise how long an activity has been happening. The activity may or may not be complete. ☐
>
> **b** talk generally about situations or activities that started in the past and are still continuing now. ☐
>
> **c** talk about situations or activities that have stopped but have a result in the present. ☐

3 **Choose the correct words.**

1 He's been *talking / talked* on the phone all morning.

2 I've *being / been* playing this game for hours now.

3 My dad *hasn't / haven't* been feeling well for a few days.

4 They've *been / being* studying since 10 o'clock.

5 We *haven't / hasn't* been living here for very long.

6 The dog's been *barked / barking* for half an hour.

4 **Complete the sentences. Use the correct form of the words and *for* or *since*.**

1 We're tired because we _____ (run) _____ hours.

2 I _____ (wait) for her _____ 40 minutes!

3 He _____ (watch) TV _____ 9 am.

4 She's red because she _____ (lie) in the sun _____ this morning.

5 They _____ (walk) in the rain _____ an hour and they're really wet.

6 Dad's exhausted because he _____ (work) in the garden _____ he got up.

50

> ## Pronunciation
> been: strong /biːn/ and weak /bɪn/
> **Go to page 120.** 🔊

5 **SPEAKING** Work in pairs. Find out how long your partner has been doing these things.

1 living in their house?   4 walking?

2 learning English?   5 talking?

3 going to school?   6 playing an instrument?

> *How long have you been playing the drums?*

> *For two years.*

Workbook page 46 ▶

VOCABULARY
Making music

1 **Complete the story of Dymonde with the verbs in the list.**

won | start | entered | released | enter
downloading | writes | record | going | playing

Alan Bolan is a musician. He ¹_____ songs. One day he decided to ²_____ *a band,* so he put an advert in the paper. He soon found the band mates he was looking for. They practised hard and started ³_____ *local gigs.* A few months ago they decided to ⁴_____ *a talent show.* They ⁵_____ *the competition,* and their prize was a day in a recording studio. They used it to ⁶_____ *a single* called *Love Me Never.* They ⁷_____ *the single* on their website two weeks ago, and loads of people have been ⁸_____ *it.* It's already ⁹_____ *the charts.* Radio stations have been playing it loads, too. Next month they are ¹⁰_____ *on tour* all over the country. Rock critics are predicting a big future for Dymonde.

2 **SPEAKING** Work in pairs. Ask your partner about their favourite band. Use the expressions in Exercise 1.

> *Who writes the songs?*

> *Have you downloaded any of their songs?*

Workbook page 48 ▶

WRITING

Write the story of your favourite band.

Write about:

- how they started.
- how long they have been together.
- how they became successful.
- some of their famous hits.
- how long you have liked them.
- why you like them.

LISTENING

1 🔊 1.38 **Listen to the interview with Tom. What is he talking about?**

2 🔊 1.38 **Listen again and circle the correct answers. Sometimes there is more than one correct answer.**

1 How does Tom feel when he hears a good new band?
   A really excited
   B worried
   C happy

2 Where does Tom hear new music?
   A on the radio
   B on the Internet
   C from his friends

3 Where does Tom get music?
   A He downloads it.
   B He borrows it from his friends.
   C He buys CDs.

4 When does he listen to music?
   A before he falls asleep
   B when he takes a shower
   C when he does his homework

5 How does Tom feel when he dances?
   A silly
   B happy
   C He doesn't dance.

3 🔊 1.39 **Now listen to Sara answering the same questions and complete the sentences.**

1 Sara mostly listens to …
2 Sara hears new music …
3 She downloads …
4 She always listens to music when …
5 When she dances she feels …

■ THiNK SELF-ESTEEM ■

Music and me

1 **Do the quiz.**

2 SPEAKING **Work in pairs. Discuss the quiz.**

- Do you agree or disagree with your score? Why?
- What music do you listen to when you are sad?
- What songs have special memories for you?
- What are your favourite song lyrics?
- How do you choose what clothes to buy?
- What music do your friends like?

Does music rock your world? Could you live without it?

Take our quiz and find out just how important music is in your life.

For each question, choose the sentence that describes you best. Then work out your score and find out just how music mad you are.

1
   A I only listen to music when I'm happy.
   B Music makes me feel better when I'm feeling down.
   C I listen to different music depending on how I feel.

2
   A I have loads of memories connected to different songs.
   B I never listen to music from when I was younger.
   C I get bored with songs quickly.

3
   A My musical taste influences the clothes I wear.
   B Music has nothing to do with fashion.
   C I don't really think about what I wear.

4
   A I have the same musical tastes as my best friends.
   B I like different music from most of my friends.
   C I always know if I'm going to be friends with someone when they tell me their taste in music.

5
   A I always listen to the lyrics in songs.
   B Melody is more important than lyrics.
   C Melody and lyrics are both really important in a song.

5–8: Music doesn't rule your world. You like it and you probably listen to it, but it's not so important.

9–11: Music plays an important part in your life, but it isn't the only thing that matters.

12–15: Music is your world and you would find it difficult to live without it. You live, sleep and breathe music.

Key
Q1 A – 1 B – 2 C – 3
Q2 A – 3 B – 2 C – 1
Q3 A – 3 B – 1 C – 2
Q4 A – 1 B – 3 C – 2
Q5 A – 1 B – 2 C – 3

READING

1 **SPEAKING** Work in pairs. How important are these things if you want to be a pop star? Put them in order 1–6. What other things can you think of?

- ☐ musical talent
- ☐ good looks
- ☐ a good manager
- ☐ luck
- ☐ loyal fans
- ☐ good songs

2 Read the article quickly. Which of these things does John Otway have?

John Otway – Rock's greatest failure

John Otway has been playing music and making records in the UK for more than 40 years. Over the years he has released more than ten albums. He has played hundreds of concerts. He has written two autobiographies. He has worked with some of the country's best musicians and he has even made a film about his life. But despite all of this, most people have never heard of him.

Otway released his first record in 1972, but it was the punk movement a few years later that really gave him his big chance. Otway wasn't the greatest musician but his songs were always fun, and his performances on stage were always entertaining – there was a good chance he would fall off the stage at least once in each show. The punks liked him, and in 1977 he had a small hit when his single *Really Free* made it to #27 in the UK top 40 charts. Otway really enjoyed his success but unfortunately, no more came. Not one of his records over the next 30 years was a hit.

Although he never had much commercial success, Otway had a lot of very loyal fans. When someone asked him what he would like for his 50th birthday, his reply was: 'A second hit.' His fans went out and bought as many copies of the new single *Bunsen Burner* as they could. And in October 2002, Otway finally saw his wish come true. In a chart that featured international superstars like Pink, Will Young and Oasis, *Bunsen Burner* made it to #9. Many high street shops refused to sell the record, saying that Otway was too old and unattractive for the teenage market. Otway didn't care. He celebrated his success with an appearance on TV's biggest music show *Top of the Pops*.

These days John Otway continues to play his music around the country, and there are always plenty of people who are happy to go and watch him perform. He's a great example for anyone who loves making music. You don't have to be young, good-looking (or even very talented) to enjoy a long career in the music business.

3 Read the article again. For each question, mark the correct answer A, B, C or D.

1 Which sentence best describes John Otway's popularity in the UK?
   - A Many people do not know his name.
   - B Everyone knows his name.
   - C He was popular 30 years ago but he isn't popular any more.
   - D He's quite popular with a lot of old people.

2 Which sentence best describes John Otway as a musician and performer?
   - A He's a very talented song writer and guitarist.
   - B He enjoys performing and making music.
   - C He's a punk.
   - D He's good at writing hit singles.

3 Why did some shops not sell his single *Bunsen Burner*?
   - A Because they thought it was terrible
   - B Because it wasn't a very big hit
   - C Because John Otway didn't want them to have it
   - D Because they thought no one would buy it

4 What is the message of the text?
   - A You don't have to be young to be a successful pop star.
   - B It's important to be successful.
   - C Do what you love doing.
   - D Musicians get better as they get older.

GRAMMAR
Present perfect simple vs. present perfect continuous

1 **Complete the sentences with the verb *play* in the correct tense. Look at the article on page 52 to check your answers.**

1 He _____ music for more than 40 years.

2 He _____ hundreds of concerts.

2 **Complete the rules and match them with the examples sentences in Exercise 1.**

> **RULES:**
> - Use the present perfect _____ to talk about an action that is not finished. ☐
> - Use the present perfect _____ to stress the *finished result* of a completed activity and the *amount* completed. ☐

3 **Complete the sentences with the phrases in the list.**

've been having | Has ... been preparing
've been watching | 've eaten | haven't taken
've played | 've been playing | 's been writing
's written | 's made

1 Sarah _____ more than 200 poems. She _____ poems since she was eight.

2 I _____ piano lesson for three years. I _____ any piano exams yet.

3 I _____ football since I was five. I _____ for three different teams.

4 We _____ films all evening. We _____ three bags of popcorn between us.

5 Mum _____ more than 100 sandwiches. _____ she _____ for the party all morning?

4 **Complete the sentences using the correct forms of the verbs.**

1 He _____ autographs since he was ten. He _____ over 500. (collect)

2 Jade _____ over 5,000 photos on her phone. She _____ them ever since she bought it. (take)

3 Mum _____ since 6 am. She _____ over 400 km. (drive)

4 We _____ for an hour. We _____ more than 2 km! (swim)

5 Mr Bosworth _____ more than 2,000 children. He _____ since he was 22. (teach)

6 They _____ apples all day. They _____ hundreds! (pick)

Workbook page 47 ▶

VOCABULARY
Musical instruments

1 **Match the instruments with the words in the list. Write 1–8 in the boxes.**

1 drums | 2 bass guitar | 3 saxophone | 4 piano
5 violin | 6 trumpet | 7 keyboard | 8 guitar

2 **◀)) 1.40 Listen. Which instrument is playing?**

1 *bass guitar*

Workbook page 48 ▶

SPEAKING

Work in pairs. Answer the questions.

1 Do you play an instrument? If yes, how long have you been playing it? If no, would you like to play an instrument?

2 Which of the instruments in Exercises 1 and 2 do you really like? Which instruments don't you like?

3 What famous musicians can you think of? How long have they been playing music? Have you seen them playing live?

Pop in the park

1 **Look at the photos and answer the questions.**

1 What's Luke's problem?

2 What suggestions do Megan and Ryan make?

2 🔊 1.41 **Now read and listen to the photostory. Check your answers.**

1

MEGAN Have a look at this. There's going to be a concert in our park.

OLIVIA Wow – The Unwanted! I've just heard their new song. I love it.

RYAN And Daddy D – awesome! I'm so going to go.

MEGAN Me, too. I can't wait.

2

OLIVIA What's up, Luke? Aren't you excited?

LUKE Not really. Well I am, but…

RYAN What? What's the matter?

LUKE I'm just a bit upset. I mean, where am I going to get £20 from? I've run out of money. I spent all my money for the month on that new video game I told you about.

3

MEGAN Can't you ask your dad?

LUKE No way. He won't lend me money. Especially for a concert. He hates my music.

OLIVIA Tell me about it. My parents can't stand my music, either.

RYAN But listen, why don't you sell something?

LUKE I haven't got anything I want to sell.

OLIVIA Nothing at all?

LUKE No, nothing.

4

LUKE Well, there's no point in getting upset. I can't go and that's that.

RYAN Well, if you say so.

OLIVIA Come on, Luke. I'm sure we'll sort something out.

RYAN This cat's been following us for ages. Hey, kitty!

MEGAN She's so cute. But you'll have to stay here now. You can't come to school with us.

DEVELOPING SPEAKING

3 Work in pairs. Discuss what happens next in the story. Write down your ideas.

We think that Ryan finds some money in the street and gives it to Luke.

4 ▶️ EP3 Watch to find out how the story continues.

5 Complete the sentences with the names in the list. There are two extra names.

Sophie | Lucky | Tiddles | Sammy | Tiger | Lucy

1 Ryan thinks the cat's name should be _____ .
2 Olivia calls the cat _____ .
3 Luke calls the cat _____ .
4 The cat's real name is _____ .

6 Why do the kids choose those names?

PHRASES FOR FLUENCY

1 Find the expressions 1–6 in the story. Who says them? How do you say them in your language?

1 I can't wait.
2 What's up?
3 No way.
4 Tell me about it.
5 There's no point in …
6 If you say so.

2 Complete the conversations. Use the expressions in Exercise 1.

1 A Hey Mandy. ¹_____ ?
  B I'm tired! I had problems with the homework last night.
  A ²_____ ! I took four hours to finish it! And I think I got some things wrong.
  B Me too. Oh well. ³_____ worrying about it. Let's give it to the teacher, and see.
2 A The Cup Final's on TV tonight. ⁴_____ !
  B I know. It's really exciting. Do you want to come and watch it with me, at my house?
  A ⁵_____ ! Your television's terrible.
  B Well, ⁶_____ . But I think our TV's really good.

WordWise
Phrasal verbs with *out*

1 Complete each of these sentences from the unit so far with a word from the list.

come | find | run | went | started | sort

1 Lots of famous musicians _____ **out** playing on the streets of London.
2 His fans _____ **out** and bought all the copies.
3 Their new single has just _____ **out**.
4 Come on, Luke. I'm sure we'll _____ something **out**.
5 I've _____ **out** of money.
6 Listen and _____ **out** how the story ends.

2 Match the phrases and the definitions.

1 start out   a discover
2 find out   b begin your working life
3 go out   c leave your house
4 come out   d appear in a shop so people can buy it
5 run out   e find an answer or solution to a problem
6 sort out   f use all of something

3 Complete the sentences with the correct form of the verbs in Exercise 2.

1 John isn't here. He _____ about 20 minutes ago.
2 It's a really old film. I think it _____ about 2005.
3 We need to go to the supermarket – we _____ of milk.
4 The police are trying to _____ who started the trouble last night.
5 We had some problems with the computer, but we _____ them _____ yesterday.
6 She's a famous singer now, but she _____ as a dancer.

Workbook page 49 ➤

FUNCTIONS
Asking about feelings

1 Match the questions and the answers.

1 What's up Luke?   a Not great.
2 Is something the matter? b Yes, I'm fine.
3 How are you feeling?   c Nothing.
4 Are you OK?   d I'm just a bit upset.

Helpful suggestions

2 ROLE PLAY Work in pairs. Student A: go to page 127. Student B: go to page 128. Look at the role cards and do the role play.

6 MAKING A DIFFERENCE

OBJECTIVES

FUNCTIONS: expressing surprise and enthusiasm

GRAMMAR: *will (not)*, *may (not)*, *might (not)* for prediction; first conditional; *unless* in first conditional sentences

VOCABULARY: the environment; verbs to talk about energy

READING

1 Match the words and phrases in the list with the pictures. Write 1–6 in the boxes.

1 a beautiful beach | 2 a dirty beach
3 clean water | 4 an attractive landscape
5 an endangered species | 6 a polluted river

2 SPEAKING Work in pairs. Which of the above are easy / difficult / impossible to find in your town or country? Discuss using the expressions below.

- There is / are lots of … in …
- I think 50 years ago there were more / fewer …
- It would be good to have more …

3 SPEAKING Tell your partner about places you have visited. Which of the things in Exercise 1 did you see?

> Years ago I visited …
>
> I saw lots of …
>
> I was surprised / disappointed to see …

4 ◀)) 1.42 Look at the sentences below about the environment. Read and listen to the article to decide if each sentence is correct or incorrect. If it's correct, mark it A. If it's incorrect, mark it B.

1 Black rhinos are far more endangered than tigers. ☐

2 At the beginning of the last century there were ten times more tigers than now. ☐

3 The fishing industry gets more money for fish that are in danger than for the ones that are not. ☐

4 The fishing laws are very strict, and the fishing industry keeps to them. ☐

5 Financial interests play a big role in deforestation. ☐

6 Sea levels rise as sea temperatures fall. ☐

5 Rewrite the false sentences from Exercise 4 to make them true.

A ☐

B ☐

C ☐

D ☐

E ☐

F ☐

Hot topic: THE ENVIRONMENT

This week, four experts share with us what they think the key challenges for the world's environment will be in the future. As always, we are curious to get our readers' reactions. So tell us what you think.

1 Endangered species

The black rhino in Africa is in serious danger of becoming extinct. This is because some people think rhino horn has special powers. They pay enormous sums of money for it. So people kill rhinos and sell their horns. Tigers are in serious danger, too. At the beginning of the 20th century, there were about 100,000 tigers. Now there are only about 3,000 left. In a few years' time, there might not be any tigers left at all! These are just two examples. Many other animals are endangered, too. Some of them may be gone forever very soon. *Joc Wagner, Cape Town*

2 Overfishing

It's not looking good for the fish population. Certain species are in danger, and there aren't many of them in the sea where fishermen usually go. Fishing ships are therefore going further and further out into the oceans. They try to get the rare species because they can get better prices for them. If things go on like this, 40 years from now there won't be any fish left in the seas. It's not too late yet, but it may be soon. The oceans need much stricter laws and a fishing industry that keeps to them. *Rick Cavendish, San Diego*

3 Deforestation

About 30% of the world's land is still covered with forests. But every year, we lose areas as big as the country of Panama. Big companies earn millions from producing wood, paper and cardboard from the trees. Forests are also cut down to make more space for growing crops such as soya or creating huge cattle farms. The consequences of deforestation are dramatic and partly responsible for climate change. About 70% of the world's land animals and plants live in forests. If we lose the forests, we will lose millions of species. *Alejandro Silvas, Quito*

4 Rising levels of sea water

Over the last 20 years or so, sea water temperatures have been going up. As a consequence, the ice caps around the poles have started to melt, and sea levels have started to rise. If this doesn't stop, the water will rise further and may flood many islands. Then some countries like the Maldives won't be there any more. There is also a danger that some huge low-lying coastal cities might end up below the sea. It's hard to imagine what the consequences of such changes might be. *Gajkaran Sanu, New Delhi*

■ THiNK VALUES ■

Caring for the world

1 **Read and tick (✓) the values that are linked with the problems discussed in the article.**

☐ 1 We have responsibilities towards future generations.

☐ 2 People have a right to express their opinions freely.

☐ 3 All people have a right to live in peace.

☐ 4 Our behaviour can make a difference.

☐ 5 Humans have a responsibility to protect endangered species.

☐ 6 We must change our behaviour towards our planet.

2 **SPEAKING Work in pairs. Say what you think about the values.**

> I think number ... is an important value.

> It says ... and I agree that ... . Do you agree?

> Yes. If we don't ... , then future generations will/won't ...

> Politicians/People/Everybody should ...

> I think it's good that ...

GRAMMAR

will (not), may (not), might (not) for prediction

1 **Complete the examples from the article on page 57. Underline other examples of *will*, *won't*, *may (not)* and *might (not)*. Then complete the rule.**

1 In a few years' time, there _____ any tigers left.

2 Some animals _____ forever very soon.

3 If we lose the forests, we _____ millions of species.

> **RULE:** Use *will* or [1]_____ to express future certainty, and [2]_____ *(not)* or *might (not)* to express future possibility.

2 **Complete the sentences. Use *will* or *won't* and the verbs in brackets.**

1 I'm not exactly sure, but I think she _____ (be) home by eight o'clock at the latest.

2 I wonder if people _____ (live) on other planets in the future.

3 I'm worried about him coming with us. I'm sure he _____ (like) any of the people at the party.

4 Who do you think _____ (win) the next World Cup?

5 It's getting cloudy. Do you think it _____ (start) raining soon?

6 Oh, don't worry about my parents. I'm sure they _____ (be) angry.

3 **Read the sentences and circle the correct words.**

1 Don't worry I *will / might* pick you up at 7.

2 The weather's a real problem. We *may / may not* be able to go for a walk.

3 She's not feeling well at all. She *might / might not* have to stay at home.

4 It *may / may not* be cold later so take a jumper with you.

5 It's my dad's birthday tomorrow. My wife and I are going to visit him, so we definitely *won't / might not* be here.

6 I'd like to get up and watch the sunrise with you, but I *may / won't* just sleep instead.

4 **SPEAKING** **Work in pairs. Think about your next weekend. Talk about:**

- a sport you will / won't do
- someone you may / may not see
- a film you might / might not watch

Workbook page 54 ➤

VOCABULARY

The environment

1 **Match the words with their definitions.**

1	extinct	a	official rules that say what people are allowed and not allowed to do
2	laws	b	to change from solid to liquid (for example, from ice to water)
3	waste	c	a large amount of water covering an area that is usually dry
4	melt	d	not existing any more
5	flood	e	things that make water, air, and the ground unclean
6	pollution	f	material that people throw away because they do not want or need it any more

2 **SPEAKING** **Work in pairs. Ask and answer questions.**

1 Which animals do you know that are extinct or in danger of extinction?

2 What laws to protect the environment are there in your country?

3 What problems with waste are there where you live?

4 What might happen if the ice around the north and south poles melts?

5 Are floods common in your country?

6 Are the air and water very polluted in your area? What could your class do to help fight pollution?

3 **◀)) 1.43** **Match the words in the list with the pictures. Write 1–4 in the boxes. Then listen, repeat and check.**

1 smog | 2 recycling | 3 litter | 4 rubbish

 A
 B
 C
 D

4 **Think about the environment in your country. Make notes.**

some rivers polluted
air pollution from factories

5 SPEAKING Work in pairs. Look at your notes from Exercise 4. Make predictions for the next 30 years. Which environmental issues concern you the most? Then report to the class.

> *Some of the rivers in our country are polluted, for example ... We think this will create big problems for the fish, and ...*

> *In some parts of the country, for example in ... , the air is polluted. We think this will change. There will be stricter laws so there won't be ...*

Workbook page 56

LISTENING

1 Read the headlines in the online newspaper story and look at the images. Write down six words you might find in the article.

Incredible Edible

Carrots in the car park

Radishes on the roundabout

The deliciously eccentric story of the town growing ALL its own vegetables.

2 🔊 1.44 You are going to listen to a story about a town named Todmorden. Use the information from the newspaper story and your imagination to say what you think is special about it. Then listen and check.

3 🔊 1.44 Listen again and answer the questions.

1 What's the project 'Incredible Edible' all about?
2 Who takes part in the project?
3 Who had the idea?
4 How did they get the idea?
5 How did people react?

4 Do you think the experiment will last? Why or why not? Would you like to see a similar experiment in your town or neighbourhood?

FUNCTIONS
Expressing surprise and enthusiasm

1 🔊 1.44 Listen to the radio programme again. The phrases below can be used to express enthusiasm. Tick the ones that the reporter uses.

☐ What a brilliant idea!
☐ That sounds wonderful!
☐ How exciting!
☐ That's amazing! (wonderful! etc.)
☐ Wow!
☐ Oh, really?
☐ Incredible! (Cool! Fascinating! etc.)

2 Put the dialogue in order. Read it out with a partner.

☐ A He has offered me a role in his next film.
☐ A I'm only going to meet Stephen Spielberg.
1 A I'm going to California this summer.
☐ A Three hours.
☐ B Cool!
☐ B Oh, really? Only three hours. Why's that?
☐ B How exciting! What are you going to talk about?
☐ B Wow! That sounds exciting. How long are you going to stay there?

3 SPEAKING Practise dialogues with a partner. A says something surprising, B reacts using one of the expressions from Exercise 1 and asks a question. A says something surprising again, etc. Use your own ideas, or the ones here.

- go to the moon
- meet Bradley Cooper
- have an important meeting
- see an alien
- only eat white food
- stay up all night

■ TRAIN TO THiNK ■

Different perspectives

1 Read these different texts. Match them with the text types in the list. Write numbers 1–4. Give your reasons. There are two text types you don't need to use.

note ☐   newspaper article ☐
diary entry ☐ informative leaflet ☐
text message ☐ adventure story ☐

2 **SPEAKING** Work in pairs. Discuss who the texts are for and what their purpose is.

> I think text 1 is probably for ...
> I think somebody wrote it in order to ...

1 This morning we took part in the Incredible Edible project. I was so proud when I saw that all of the 27 children in my class had brought vegetable plants ...

2 Meeting the guys who want to plant vegetables by the football field at 5... Hope to CUL8R. S.

3 ... to buy OUR vegetables. They come from local farms in the neighbourhood. They are organic and fresh – and you don't have to pick them yourself. Prices are reasonable, the quality is high!

4 Reporter Mac Hendon has learned that the council will soon publish a list of spare land that can be used by the Incredible Edible project. It has been ...

READING

1 Read the text. What type of text is it? Choose from the types in the exercise above. Who might this text be for?

Small changes, BIG consequences
6 things you can do to help the environment

1. Don't leave your DVD player, your computer or other electrical appliances on standby. If you switch off your TV completely when you've stopped watching, it won't use any electricity. People think that a gadget on standby uses only the electricity for that 'little red light'. Not true!

2. When you charge your mobile, disconnect the charger from the phone when the battery is fully charged. Otherwise you're wasting energy.

3. If you reuse your shopping bags when you go to the supermarket, you'll save money. If you keep them and take them with you the next time you go shopping, you won't need new bags. Don't forget that a lot of energy is needed to produce plastic bags, and plastic waste is a danger for the environment. Unless people stop throwing plastic away, the environment will suffer even more.

4. Don't let the water run while you're brushing your teeth. If you turn it off and use a cup of water to rinse your mouth, you'll save a lot of water!

5. Make sure none of the taps in your house drip. If a tap drips, it wastes three or more litres of water a day.

6. Think before you throw things away, and tell your family to do the same. They may not want to use an old mobile, computer or MP3 player any more. That doesn't mean those things should end up in the litter bin. If they go to a charity instead, other people might find them very useful.

2 **SPEAKING** Work in pairs. Cover up the text and try to complete the sentences.

1 A gadget on standby uses ...
2 When your phone is fully charged you should ...
3 Plastic bags are a problem for the environment because ... So we should ...
4 When you brush your teeth it's better to ...
5 Taps should never ...
6 Before you throw something away, ask yourself who might ...

3 Read the tips again. Which of the suggestions ...

- do you already do?
- would be easy for you to start doing?
- would be difficult for you to follow?

GRAMMAR
First conditional; *unless* in first conditional sentences

1 **Complete the sentences with the correct form of the verbs. Look at the leaflet on page 60 and check your answers. Then choose the right answers to make the rules.**

1 If you switch off your TV completely when you have stopped watching, it _____ (not use) any electricity.

2 If you reuse your shopping bags when you go to the supermarket, you _____ (save) money.

3 Unless people stop throwing plastic away, the environment _____ (suffer) even more.

> **RULE:** We use the first conditional to talk about the consequences of a [1]*possible / impossible* future action.
> - Condition clause: *if* + present simple
> - Result clause: *will / won't* + main verb
>
> The condition clause can come before or after the result clause.
>
> *Unless* means [2]*only if / if not.*

2 **Match the parts of the sentences.**

1 Unless someone lends me a bit of money, ☐
2 I'll only be able to go to the concert ☐
3 They won't pass the exam ☐
4 Won't she miss the train ☐

a if my dad drives me there.
b if she doesn't leave for the station now?
c I won't be able to take the bus home.
d unless they study hard.

3 **Write first conditional sentences. Then decide in which of them you could use *unless*.**

0 environment / suffer / if / we not recycle more
The environment will suffer if we don't recycle more. The environment will suffer unless we recycle more.

1 if / I give this phone / charity / they find someone who needs it

2 if / this tap not stop dripping / how much water / we waste in a day?

3 situation / become worse / if they not change behaviour

4 Look – battery full! / if you not disconnect charger / you waste energy

5 if she read this book / she understand situation better

6 if / you not stop shouting / I not listen any more

4 **Complete the questions. Use the correct form of the verbs.**

0 What _will_ you _do_ if they _don't help_ you? (do / not help)

1 If you _____, _____ you _____ good marks in your test? (not study / get)

2 Unless the weather _____ really bad on Sunday, we _____ to the beach. (be / go)

3 If she _____ you to her birthday party, _____ you _____ her a present? (invite / buy)

4 She _____ him unless he _____ her very nicely. (not help / ask)

5 If I _____ to visit you, _____ you _____ me around your town? (come / show)

5 **SPEAKING** **Work in pairs. Ask and answer questions using the first conditional. Use your own ideas or the ones here.**

1 What will you do if it rains all weekend?

2 What will you buy if you get some extra money this month?

3 What will you do tonight if you don't have any homework?

> Workbook page 55 ▶

VOCABULARY
Verbs to talk about energy

1 **◀)) 2.02** **Match the verbs with their definitions. Write 1–8. Listen and check.**

1 to reuse | 2 to throw away | 3 to recycle
4 to waste | 5 to charge | 6 to disconnect
7 to save | 8 to leave on standby

a not to switch an appliance off completely so it is ready to be used at any time ☐

b to collect and treat rubbish in order to produce useful materials that can be used again ☐

c to fill up an empty battery again ☐

d to get rid of something ☐

e to stop something from being wasted ☐

f to stop the connection between an electrical appliance and the power source ☐

g to use something again ☐

h to use too much of something or use it incorrectly ☐

2 **SPEAKING** **Work in pairs. Discuss these questions.**

1 Do you waste a lot of energy? What could you do to save energy?

2 What things do you reuse?

3 What things do you recycle? Do you think there is enough recycling done where you live? Why?

> Workbook page 56 ▶

Culture

1 Look at the picture. Do you know what this is?

2 **◀)) 2.03** Read and listen to the article. What animals does it mention?

STOP! BEFORE IT'S TOO LATE

The Himalayas

Why should we care?

The Himalayan mountains in South Central Asia contain many of the world's tallest **peaks**, including Mount Everest. They also contain the biggest number of **glaciers** after the North and South poles. Three of the greatest rivers in the world start from these mountains: the Ganges, the Indus and the Yangtze. These rivers provide water to a billion people in Asia.

What's happening?

The biggest danger to the Himalayas is **global warming**, which is melting the glaciers fast. There is also a huge problem with deforestation in the mountains. Many species of animals such as the tiger, the rhino and the snow leopard are in danger.

The Galapagos Islands

Why should we care?

The Galapagos Islands are one of the most amazing places on Earth. These **tiny** islands are 1,000 km from Ecuador in the Pacific, and contain many species of plants and animals that are found nowhere else in the world, among them the giant tortoise, the Galapagos penguin and the Galapagos sea lion. They are also famous because the scientist Charles Darwin spent time there studying the wildlife.

What's happening?

The Galapagos Islands are very **fragile**. The greatest dangers to them include overfishing, pollution and tourism. There is also a threat of animals from other parts of the world arriving on the islands and killing the local wildlife.

The Amazon

Why should we care?

The Amazon in Brazil is the largest tropical rainforest in the world. It is home to 10% of the world's wildlife. The Amazon River is the largest in the world and contains the most freshwater fish on the planet. It is also home to 350 different **tribes**. But perhaps most importantly, it provides between 25 and 30% of the world's oxygen.

What's happening?

The biggest **threat** is deforestation. This happens to make space for farm land and to have wood. As a result, many animals are endangered, among them the golden lion tamarin and the jaguar. Since 1950 we have lost more than 17% of the Amazon rainforest. We can't afford to lose any more.

The Great Barrier Reef

Why should we care?

The Great Barrier Reef, off the eastern coast of Australia, is over 2,000 km long. It is the only living **organism** on the planet that you can see from space. It is home to 1,500 different types of fish, 400 different types of coral, 215 different types of birds and six different types of turtle.

What's happening?

We have already lost 10% of all the coral, but scientists **fear** that we will lose 70% more in the next 40 years. The greatest dangers to the reef are pollution and overfishing.

3 SPEAKING Work in pairs. Say what these numbers in the article refer to.

a 1,000,000,000 d 1,000
b 350 e 2,000
c 17 f 70

A billion — that's the number of people in Asia that get their water from the Ganges, the Indus and the Yangtze.

4 SPEAKING Can you think of any other areas of the world that are in danger from environmental damage?

5 VOCABULARY **Match the words in bold in the article with the definitions. Write the words.**

0 groups of people who live together, usually outside towns and cities, and have the same language, culture, and history *tribes*

1 the rise in temperature of the Earth's climate _____

2 a living thing _____

3 are afraid _____

4 weak / easy to damage _____

5 large masses of ice that move slowly _____

6 the tops of mountains _____

7 very small _____

8 something that will probably harm or destroy something else _____

> **Pronunciation**
> /f/, /v/, /b/ consonant sounds
> **Go to page 120.**

WRITING
An article for the school magazine

1 Read this article from a school magazine. Answer the questions.

1 What is its purpose?

2 How has the river changed?

3 What are the main reasons for the problems?

4 What will happen if the situation doesn't change?

5 What should be done?

2 Put the words in the correct order to make sentences from the article. Then go through it and underline the evidence the writer uses to support each of these statements.

1 so / the / beautiful / once / Quiller River / was

2 situation / alarming / is / the

3 the / river / and / look at / banks / just

3 Match the sentence halves. Which of them talk about possible consequences? Which are suggestions? Which are predictions?

1 If politicians wake up and we all do something,

2 We need stricter laws

3 In a few years' time

4 So I really think politicians

5 The situation will be even worse in a few years

a to protect our river.

b unless factories stop polluting.

c we might once again be able to enjoy the river.

d should do something about it.

e all the fish may be dead.

4 The article has four paragraphs. Which of them …

a expresses the writer's hope that the situation will be better in the future?

b introduces the topic?

c describes problems and says what should be done?

d describes problems, says what will happen if nothing is done and what should be done?

The sad story of a once beautiful river

The Quiller River was once so beautiful that there is even a song about it. And now?

The situation is alarming. There are lots of factories along the river. Newspapers have recently reported that the water in the river is totally polluted. There are hardly any fish left, and the water itself smells terrible. The situation will be even worse in a few years unless factories stop polluting the water. So I really think politicians should do something about it. We need stricter laws to protect our river.

And just look at the river banks. They are covered in litter. It seems that there are lots of people who throw their waste into the river. This must stop! We should all get together and help clean up the river banks.

If politicians wake up and we all do something, we might once again be able to enjoy the beauty of the river. Let's hope it's not too late.

5 Choose one of these environmental problems and make notes about what the situation is now, possible consequences and what should be done.

a one of the problems mentioned in this unit, for example, deforestation in the Amazon

b an environmental issue in your town or country

6 Write an article for your school magazine raising awareness about the environmental issue you have chosen.

- Find a good title.
- Write an introduction that catches the reader's interest.
- Describe what the problems are, what you think the consequences might be and what should be done.

CAMBRIDGE ENGLISH: Preliminary

◼ THiNK EXAMS ◼

READING
Part 5: Four-option multiple-choice cloze

1   Read the text below and choose the correct word for each space.
    For each question, mark the correct letter A, B, C or D.

I'm an eco-counsellor at my school. It's a job I have 0_____ doing for 6 months, and it's something I enjoy a lot. As an eco-counsellor I'm responsible 1_____ making sure that our school does as much 2_____ it can for our environment.

Altogether there are six of us. We have 3_____ meeting once every two weeks, and we discuss what we can do 4_____ encourage students to think about their behaviour and how to be more environmentally friendly. For example, last month we 5_____ a plan to stop littering around the school. We put up posters 6_____ , and I even made a small speech in a school assembly. It's already had an amazing impact, and you 7_____ ever see any rubbish on the floor in a the school. We 8_____ decided to get students to think about recycling. We have now got different bins for glass, paper and plastics in 9_____ classroom. If we all 10_____ the bins, our school will be a cleaner, healthier place.

0	A being	B be	C been (circled)	D was
1	A for	B of	C in	D by
2	A so	B than	C for	D as
3	A a	B –	C an	D the
4	A for	B to	C so	D about
5	A did	B made	C ran	D make
6	A everywhere	B nowhere	C anywhere	D somewhere
7	A often	B sometimes	C hardly	D occasionally
8	A too	B also	C as well	D else
9	A all	B some	C every	D no
10	A using	B have used	C are using	D use

WRITING
Part 1: Sentence transformations

Workbook page 17 ➤

2   Here are some sentences about music.
    For each question, complete the second sentence so it means the same as the first.
    Use no more than three words.

0   We moved into this house two years ago.
    We ____*have been*____ living in this house for two years.

1   Their new CD isn't as good as the last one.
    Their last CD was _____ their new one.

2   Two hours ago he got into the pool and started swimming.
    He _____ for two hours.

3   If you don't practise, you'll never be a good drummer.
    You won't be a good drummer _____ practise.

4   They came on stage at 8 pm and they're still playing now two hours later.
    They _____ on stage for two hours now.

5   There a 50% chance that I'll go to the show on Saturday.
    I _____ to the show on Saturday.

TEST YOURSELF

VOCABULARY

1 **Complete the sentences with the words in the list. There are two extra words.**

release | standby | tour | extinct | flood | record
enter | waste | charge | melt | download | throw away

1 Is it OK if I _____ my mobile phone in your room?
2 It's getting warm now, so I think the snow will _____ soon.
3 Don't _____ water. You shouldn't stay in the shower for more than four minutes!
4 Our WiFi connection is really slow. It takes a long time to _____ songs.
5 They've recorded a new CD, and they're going to _____ it next week.
6 You can't win the competition if you don't _____ it!
7 After the band released their new record, they went on _____ for three months.
8 If it carries on raining like this, there might be a _____ tonight.
9 There aren't many of these animals left in the world. They could be _____ in a few years.
10 Don't switch it off completely – leave it on _____, OK?

/10

GRAMMAR

2 **Complete the sentences with the words in the list.**

unless | if | have played | have been playing | won't | might not

1 I didn't study for the test. I _____ pass it, I'm sure!
2 Sorry, Mum. My shoes are really dirty. I _____ football in the park.
3 We won't go for a walk _____ it rains.
4 I don't feel very well, so I _____ go to school tomorrow. I'm not sure.
5 I'll never finish this homework _____ you help me. Please!
6 Everyone in the team is really tired. We _____ three games this week already!

3 **Find and correct the mistake in each sentence.**

1 He's being working here for over ten years.
2 If it will rain, we'll stay at home.
3 I've been making fifty sandwiches for the party tonight.
4 We might to go out tonight.
5 You won't do well in the test unless you don't study.
6 Ouch! I've been cutting my finger.

/12

FUNCTIONAL LANGUAGE

4 **Complete the sentences with the words in the list.**

bit | doing | How | matter | news | not | sounds | up

1 A Hi Jack. What's the _____ ?
    B Nothing much. I'm just a _____ upset.
2 A What's _____ , Maria? Why are you crying?
    B I'm crying because I'm happy. I won a competition.
    A _____ exciting! I'm really happy for you.
3 A How are you _____ ?
    B Well, _____ great. But I'll be OK, I think.
4 A I've got some _____ ! We're going to get a cat.
    B That _____ great! I'm sure you're really happy.

/8

PRONUNCIATION

UNIT 1
Intonation and sentence stress

1 🔊 1.12 **Read and listen to the dialogue.**

HENRY I know … let's learn to surf!
LUCY That's a great idea!
HENRY Do you think so?
LUCY Of course! We'll need lessons.
HENRY I'll phone the surf shop!
LUCY It'll be fun… we should definitely do it!

2 **Which words show that Lucy likes Henry's idea?**

3 🔊 1.13 **Listen and repeat the dialogue.**

UNIT 2
Word stress

1 🔊 1.17 **Read and listen to the dialogue.**

SARAH Jack, I can't believe it! Do you recognise that man over there?
JACK I suppose it could be someone we know…
SARAH How could you forget? Think, Jack!
JACK Oh, yeah! Now I remember! He's on that TV quiz show.
SARAH That's right. It's called, 'Concentrate'. I wonder what he's doing here?

2 **How many syllables do the blue / red / green words have? Say these verbs, and stress the correct syllable.**

3 🔊 1.18 **Listen and repeat the dialogue.**

UNIT 3
Words ending in /ə/

1 🔊 1.22 **Read and listen to the dialogue.**

JOE Why don't we go to the cinema? We can see The Monster in the Computer. Tammy Baker plays the monster.
TESS Well… there's also River Adventure. Tom Webster's a doctor in it.
JOE I know he's a better actor than Tammy Baker but River Adventure is a lot longer. If we see the shorter film we can have dinner after.
TESS Okay; it looks much funnier, too. And let's go to the Super Burger for dinner!

2 **Say the words ending in the short /ə/ sound.**

3 🔊 1.23 **Listen and repeat the dialogue.**

UNIT 4
The short /ʌ/ vowel sound

1 🔊 1.31 **Read and listen to the poem.**

My little cousin from London's coming on Monday.
She's young and lovely – and very funny.
She loves the sun and running and jumping.
She doesn't like studying or spending money.

2 **Say the words with the /ʌ/ vowel sound in blue.**

3 🔊 1.32 **Listen and repeat the poem.**

UNIT 5
been: strong /biːn/ and weak /bɪn/

1 🔊 1.36 **Read and listen to the dialogue.**

JILL Where have you been? The party's already started.
PETE Shh! I've been hiding in the kitchen.
JILL We've been looking for you everywhere. We want to play a game.
PETE Well, I've been trying to find a bin to put this sandwich in. It's horrible!

2 **Say the strong and weak forms of** *been*, **/biːn/ and /bɪn/. What other word sounds like /bɪn/?**

3 🔊 1.37 **Listen and repeat the dialogue.**

UNIT 6
/f/, /v/ and /b/ consonant sounds

1 🔊 2.04 **Read and listen to the advertisement.**

Visit the beautiful village of Victoria!
The village is surrounded by forests and farms.
There's a fantastic river for fishing.
You can buy souvenirs and see very old buildings.
There are buses to the beach from Monday to Friday.
You'll never forget your visit to Victoria!

2 **Say the words with the /f/, /v/ and /b/ sounds.**

3 🔊 2.05 **Listen and repeat the sentences.**

This page is intentionally left blank.

UNIT 1
Present perfect vs. past simple

> Learners often use the present perfect when the past simple is required.
>
> We use the past simple to talk about events which have taken place at a specific time. We use the present perfect to talk about events where the time is not specified.
>
> ✓ *I **went** on holiday with my family last year.*
> ✗ *I ~~have been~~ on holiday with my family last year.*

Write positive answers to the following questions using the words given in the correct tense.

0 Have you started your new job? (last weekend)
Yes, I have. I started my new job last weekend.

1 Have you seen the latest episode? (yesterday)

_____

2 Have you been to France before? (two times)

_____

3 Have you visited your grandparents recently? (a few days ago)

_____

4 Have you seen John? (five minutes ago)

_____

5 Have you changed your phone? (for a better one)

_____

6 Have you earned any money recently? (over £100 last week)

_____

UNIT 2
Present perfect with *for* or *since*

> Learners often use the present simple with *for* or *since* when the present perfect is required.
>
> We use the present perfect tense with both *for* and *since* referring to an earlier time which is still relevant now.
>
> ✓ *I **have known** him for three months.*
> ✗ *I ~~know~~ him for three months.*

Make new sentences in the perfect tense using the information given.

0 I started playing the guitar when I was six years old. I still play the guitar now.
I've played the guitar since I was six years old.

1 We were friends when we were ten. We are still friends now.

_____

2 I saw her when I was five. I did not see her after that.

_____

3 I started working in the newsagent's two years ago. I work there now.

_____

4 You moved to Madrid six months ago.

_____

5 My family travelled abroad in 2010. They did not travel abroad after that.

_____

6 Have you earned any money recently? (over £100 last week)

_____

UNIT 3
Comparatives and *than*

> Learners often use the wrong forms of adjectives, trying to use *more* where it is not possible, especially with *bigger* and *cheaper*.
>
> For adjectives with one syllable, we add *-er* for the comparative.
>
> ✓ *In ten years' time my town will be **bigger** than now.*
> ✗ *In ten years' time my town will be ~~more big~~ than now.*
>
> For adjectives with two syllables ending in *-y*, we make the comparative by adding *-ier*.
>
> ✓ *I find English **easier** than French.*
> ✗ *I find English ~~more easy~~ than French.*
>
> Learners sometimes use *that* instead of *than*.
>
> ✓ *Sports clubs are much better **than** the gym.*
> ✗ *Sports clubs are much better ~~that~~ the gym.*

Correct the following sentences.

1 I am much more happy than before.

_____

2 If you go to Europe, the weather will be better in July that in February.

_____

3 Which is more old, soccer or rugby?

_____

4 The beaches are cleaner in the countryside that in the city.

_____

5 It will make you fitter and more healthy.

_____

UNIT 4
Any vs. – (no article)

> **Learners often miss out _any_ where it is needed in questions and negative statements.**
>
> ✓ Do you have **any** questions? If so, please visit me in my office.
> ✗ Do you have ⎯ questions? If so, please visit me in my office.

Circle the correct answer, _any_ or – (no article).

1 In the countryside there aren't _any_ / – discos.
2 I didn't take _any_ / – notice of it and deleted it again.
3 I have been doing _any_ / – homework.
4 We need _any_ / – time to work on this.
5 I have been here for four months and I can't live here _any_ / – longer.
6 Do you have _any_ / – money I can borrow?

will vs. should

> **Learners sometimes use _will_ instead of _should_.**
>
> **We use _should_ to give advice to someone, or to mean that something is supposed to happen.**
>
> ✓ In my opinion, the subject you **should** talk about is the environment.
> ✗ In my opinion, the subject you ~~will~~ talk about is the environment.

Circle the correct answer.

1 In my opinion, you will / _should_ not move schools.
2 If you like the seaside, you _will_ / _should_ go to the south coast.
3 If we do it that way, it _will_ / _should_ be a disaster.

4 On this diet, you must eat healthy food, and you _won't_ / _shouldn't_ drink fizzy drinks.
5 _I'll_ / _I should_ meet you there if you like.
6 _Will_ / _Should_ we study everything for the test or just this unit?

UNIT 5
Present simple or present continuous vs. present perfect continuous

> **Learners sometimes use the present simple or the present continuous when the present perfect continuous is required.**
>
> **We use the present perfect continuous to talk about how long we have been doing something. We often use it with _for_ and _since_ and a time period.**
>
> ✓ I **have been living** in this house for three years.
> ✗ I ~~live~~ in this house for three years.
> ✓ I ~~am living~~ in this house for three years.

Correct the following sentences.

1 I try to do that for ages, but I can't manage it.

_____

2 How long is Michael learning English?

_____

3 I have always been going to work by train, because I live far away.

_____

4 His friends laugh every time he is telling that joke – I don't know why.

_____

5 I need to fill in your address – where have you been living?

_____

6 Since last Wednesday I go to karate lessons.

_____

UNIT 6
Future with *will*

> **Learners sometimes use the present simple tense when the future tense is required.**
>
> ✓ We **will meet** at 9 p.m. tomorrow.
> ✗ We ~~meet~~ at 9 p.m. tomorrow.

Correct the following sentences.

1   We normally will go there every Wednesday.

_____

2   I think I will know what you mean.

_____

3   So I see you on the 15th.

_____

4   I'm sure you want to go there when you see these pictures.

_____

5   When I will get home, I'll send you a text.

_____

6   Who wins the next football match?

_____

STUDENT A

UNIT 1, PAGE 19

Student A

1   You've got an idea of how to raise money for a charity in India: Students can pay £1 and not wear their school uniform one day next week. But is it really a good idea? You're not too sure. Tell Student B your idea and see what they think.

2   Student B wants to tell you about an idea for a new school club. Listen to the idea and encourage them to do it. Offer help and maybe some ideas of your own.

UNIT 5, PAGE 55

Student A

1   You're a bit upset. There's a party at the weekend, but your mum says you can't go. Talk to your friend about the problem.

2   Your friend looks a bit upset. Find out what the problem is and see if you can help.

Why don't you …

You could …

Can't you … ?

STUDENT B

UNIT 1, PAGE 19

Student B

1   Student A wants to tell you about an idea to raise money for a charity in India. Listen to the idea and encourage them to do it. Offer help and maybe some ideas of your own.

2   You've got an idea for a new school club: a cooking club that helps students learn how to cook healthy food. But is it really a good idea? You're not too sure. Tell Student B your idea and see what they think.

UNIT 5, PAGE 55

Student B

1   Your friend looks a bit upset. Find out what the problem is and see if you can help.

   Why don't you …

   You could …

   Can't you … ?

2   You're a bit upset. It's your mum's birthday tomorrow and you haven't got any money to buy her a present. Talk to your friend about the problem.

Acknowledgements

The authors and publishers acknowledge the following sources of copyright material and are grateful for the permissions granted. While every effort has been made, it has not always been possible to identify the sources of all the material used, or to trace all copyright holders. If any omissions are brought to our notice, we will be happy to include the appropriate acknowledgements on reprinting:

James Zull for the adapted text on p. 14. Reproduced with permission;

The Department of Homeland Security for the text on p. 39 adapted from Heads Up Stop Think Connect. Copyright © Department of Homeland Security's National Cybersecurity Awareness Campaign, Stop. Think.Connect™. The Department of Homeland Security's cooperation and assistance does not reflect an endorsement of the contents of Think! Reproduced with permission;

Daily Mail for the text and listening exercise on p. 59 adapted from 'Carrots in the car park. Radishes on the roundabout. The deliciously eccentric story of the town growing all its own veg' by Vincent Graff. Daily Mail 10/12/2011. Copyright © Daily Mail;

The publishers are grateful to the following for permission to reproduce copyright photographs and material:

T = Top, B = Below, L = Left, R = Right, C = Centre, B/G = Background

p. 4 (L): ©LuckyBusiness/iStock/360/Getty Images; p. 4 (R): ©Myfanwy Jane Webb/iStock/360/Getty Images; p. 5 (TL): ©Jonathan Larsen/iStock/360/Getty Images; p. 5 (TC): ©Charles Bowman/age fotostock/Getty Images; p. 5 (TR): ©John Peter Photography/Alamy; p. 5 (BL): ©Federico Cabrera/LatinContent/Getty Images; p. 5 (BR): ©Sharron Schiefelbein/Alamy; p. 6: ©ROBYN BECK/AFP/Getty Images; p. 7 (armchair): ©murat5234/iStock/360/Getty Images; p. 7 (book shelves): ©de santis paolo/iStock/360/Getty Images; p. 7 (carpet): ©Hemera Technologies/PhotoObjects.net/360/Getty Images; p. 7 (cooker): ©ppart/iStock/360/Getty Images; p. 7 (curtains): ©Denyshutter/iStock/360/Getty Images; p. 7 (desk): ©val lawless/Shutterstock; p. 7 (lamp): ©janniwet/iStock/360/Getty Images; p. 7 (mirror): ©GaryAlvis/E+/Getty Images; p. 7 (shower cubicle): ©Sergio Stakhnyk/Shutterstock; p. 7 (sofa): ©AnnaDavy/iStock/360/Getty Images; p. 7 (toilet): ©Vladimir Konjushenko/iStock/360/Getty Images; p. 7 (wardrobe): ©igor terekhov/iStock/360/Getty Images; p. 10: ©David Cole/Alamy; p. 12 (R): ©Jupiterimages/Stockbyte/Getty Images; p. 12 (TC): ©Edler von Rabenstein/Shutterstock; p. 12 (L): ©Datacraft - Sozaijiten/Alamy; p. 12 (BC): ©Stockbyte/Getty Images; p. 13: ©Subbotina Anna/Shutterstock; p. 14 (Ex5): ©Vilmos Varga/Shutterstock; p. 15 (1a): ©Sproetniek/Vetta/Getty Images; p. 15 (1b): ©Scott Quinn Photography/Photolibrary/Getty Images; p. 15 (1c): ©Netfalls - Remy Musser/Shutterstock; p. 15 (2a): ©chris2766/iStock/360/Getty Images; p. 15 (2b): ©Ben Jeayes/Shutterstock; p. 15 (2c): ©Janne Ahvo/iStock/360/Getty Images;
p. 15 (3a): ©Timurpix/Shutterstock; p. 15 (3b): ©Ljupco/iStock/360/Getty Images;
p. 15 (3c): ©Mazur/WireImage/Getty Images; p. 15 (4a): ©Gregory Costanzo/Stone/Getty Images; p. 15 (4b): ©Zave Smith/Corbis; p. 15 (4c): ©mrkornflakes/Shutterstock; p. 15 (R): ©Olga Korneeva/Shutterstock; p. 16 (TL): ©nPine/nPine/360/Getty Images; p. 16 (TR): ©JGI/Jamie Grill/Blend Images/Getty Images; p. 16 (BL): ©imageBROKER/Alamy; p. 16 (BR): ©68/Ocean/Corbis; p. 18 (footballer): ©Sergey Nivens/Shutterstock; p. 18 (woman in blue hat): ©Rido/Shutterstock; p. 20 (TL): ©kali9/iStock/360/Getty Images; p. 20 (TR): ©Jupiterimages/Creatas/360/Getty Images; p. 20 (B): ©Fuse/Getty Images; p. 21: ©Gever Tulley/Brightworks http://sfbrightworks.org; p. 23 (TL): ©Fancy Collection/Fancy Collection/Superstock; p. 23 (TC): ©Oleh_Slobodeniuk/iStock/360/Getty Images; p. 23 (TR): ©Jupiterimages/Pixland/360/Getty Images; p. 23 (BL): ©Blue Jean Images / Blue Jean Images/Superstock; p. 23 (BR): ©Fuse/Getty Images; p. 24 (TR): ©SOVEREIGN, ISM/SCIENCE PHOTO LIBRARY; p. 26 (TR): ©Patrik Giardino/Stone/Getty Images; p. 26 (BL): ©asiseeit/Vetta/Getty Images; p. 26 (BR): ©Thinkstock/Stockbyte/Getty Images; p. 28 (1 apples): ©Anna Kucherova/Shutterstock; p. 28 (1 bread): ©Africa Studio/Shutterstock; p. 28 (1 eggs): ©Nattika/Shutterstock; p. 28 (1 milk): ©studioVin/Shutterstock; p. 28 (2 clock): ©Nikolai Sorokin/Hemera/360/Getty Images; p. 28 (3a): ©m-imagephotography/iStock/360/Getty Images; p. 28 (3b): ©Stas Perov/iStock/360/Getty Images; p. 28 (3c): ©Concept Photo/Shutterstock; p. 28 (4a): ©marco mayer/Shutterstock; p. 28 (4b): ©aquariagirl1970/Shutterstock; p. 28 (4c): ©Vereshchagin Dmitry/Shutterstock; p. 28 (5 calendar): ©Mega_Pixel/iStock/360/Getty Images; p. 30 (TL): ©Gene Chutka/E+/Getty Images; p. 30 (TR): ©Wendell Metzen/Photolibrary/Getty Images; p. 30 (CL TV show): ©REX/ITV; p. 30 (CL TV): ©ronstik/iStock/360/Getty Images; p. 30 (BL): ©Dave Parker/Alamy; p. 30 (BC): ©Pixel 4 Images/Shutterstock; p. 30 (BR): ©Elan Fleisher/LOOK/Getty Images; p. 31: ©Everett Collection/REX; p. 33: ©Sergio Schnitzler/Shutterstock; p. 34: ©Twitter; p. 35 (chat show): ©Brian J. Ritchie/Hotsauce/REX; p. 35 (drama series, cartoon, game show, reality show, soap opera): ©ITV/REX; p. 35 (news): ©Ken McKay/REX; p. 35 (sitcom): ©CBS/courtesy Everett Collection/REX; p. 35 (sports programme): ©Cal Sport Media/REX; p. 35 (talent show): ©20thC.Fox/Everett/REX; p. 38: ©Facebook; p. 38: ©Google+; p. 38: ©LinkedIn; p. 38: ©Pinterest; p. 38: ©Twitter; p. 38 (B/G): ©VKA/Shutterstock; p. 39 (TL): ©Luciano Leon/Alamy; p. 39 (BR): ©Fuse/Getty Images; p. 41: ©sturti/E+/Getty Images; p. 42 (TL): ©YanLev/Shutterstock; p. 42 (BL): ©RTimages/iStock/360/Getty Images; p. 42 (R): ©Mel-nik/Shutterstock; p. 44 (TL, B/G): ©Christie's Images/Corbis; p. 44 (R): ©The Art Archive/Alamy; p. 44 (CL): ©AleksVF/iStock/360/Getty Images; p. 44 (CR): ©Gonzalo Azumendi/The Image/Bank/Getty Images; p. 46 (Dawn): ©laindiapiaroa/iStock/360/Getty Images; p. 46 (Paula): ©Comstock Images/Stockbyte/Getty Images; p. 46 (Keith): ©Alen-D/iStock/360/Getty Images; p. 46 (Lisa): ©XiXinXing/Getty Images; p. 46 (B): ©Allies Interactive/Shutterstock; p. 48 (1): ©kzenon/iStock/360/Getty Images; p. 48 (2): ©Lonely Planet/Lonely Planet Images/Getty Images; p. 48 (3): ©Jon Feingersh/Blend Images/Getty Images; p. 48 (4): ©Comstock/Stockbyte/Getty Images; p. 48 (5): ©Andrey Armyagov/Shutterstock; p. 48 (6): ©Roxana Gonzalez/Shutterstock; p. 49 (TL): ©Creatas Images/Creatas/360/Getty Images; p. 49 (TR): ©David Fisher/REX; p. 49 (CR): ©Karwai Tang/WireImage/Getty Images; p. 49 (BR): ©Tips Images / Tips Images/Superstock; p. 50: ©Roxana Gonzalez/Shutterstock; p. 51: ©g-stockstudio/iStock/360/Getty Images; p. 52: ©Hayley Madden/Redferns/Getty Images; p. 56 (a): ©Jiri Balek/Shutterstock; p. 56 (b): ©amelaxa/Shutterstock; p. 56 (c): ©Wirepec/iStock/360/Getty Images; p. 56 (d): ©srdjan draskovic/iStock/360/Getty Images; p. 56 (e): ©Simon Dannhauer/iStock/360/Getty Images; p. 56 (f): ©naumoid/iStock/360/Getty Images; p. 57 (L): ©luoman/E+/Getty Images; p. 57 (C): ©konmesa/iStock/360/Getty Images; p. 57 (R): ©John G. Wilbanks/Alamy; p. 58 (TL): ©Frank Herholdt/Alamy; p. 58 (TR): ©kanvag/iStock/360/Getty Images; p. 58 (BL): ©Gruffydd Thomas/Alamy; p. 58 (BR): ©Lou Linwei/Alamy; p. 59: ©Incredible Edible Todmorden www.incredible-edible-todmorden.co.uk; p. 62 (TR): ©Eric Gevaert/iStock/360/Getty Images; p. 62 (B/G): ©BlueOrange Studio/Shutterstock;

Commissioned photography by: Jon Barlow p 18 (1-4), 36

Cover photographs by: (TL): ©Tim Gainey/Alamy; (C): ©hugh sturrock/Alamy; (R): ©Andrea Haase/iStock/Getty Images Plus/Getty Images; (BL): ©Oliver Burston/Alamy.

The publishers are grateful to the following illustrators: Arpad Olbey (Beehive Illustration) 6, 11, 60; Bryan Beach (Advocate Art) 5, 43; David Semple 9, 14; Graham Kennedy 8, 22, 24, 32, 53

The publishers are grateful to the following contributors:
Blooberry: text design and layouts; Claire Parson: cover design; Hilary Fletcher: picture research; Leon Chambers: audio recordings; Silversun Media Group: video production; Karen Elliott: Pronunciation sections; Matt Norton: Get it right! sections

This page is intentionally left blank.

THiNK

WORKBOOK 2

B1

Herbert Puchta, Jeff Stranks & Peter Lewis-Jones

CAMBRIDGE
UNIVERSITY PRESS

This page is intentionally left blank.

CONTENTS

Welcome   4

WELCOME

A GETTING TO KNOW YOU

Asking questions

1 Put the words in order to make questions.

0 are / from / where / you

Where are you from _____ ?

1 you / 15 / are

_____ ?

2 doing / you / are / what

_____ ?

3 do / do / you / what

_____ ?

4 do / like / doing / you / what

_____ ?

5 like / you / TV / watching / do

_____ ?

2 Write the questions.

0 A *Are you 13* _____ ?

B Yes, I am. Last Saturday was my 13th birthday.

1 A _____ ?

B I'm just finishing my homework. I won't be long.

2 A _____ ?

B India, but I live in the UK.

3 A _____ ?

B Yes, I do, especially football.

4 A _____ ?

B Hanging out with my friends. That's my favourite thing.

5 A _____ ?

B I'm a teacher.

3 Answer the questions in Exercise 2 so that they are true for you.

_____

_____

_____

_____

_____

_____

The weather

1 Match the pictures and the sentences.

0 It's dry and cloudy. [F]

1 It's warm and sunny. [ ]

2 It's cold and foggy. [ ]

3 It's hot and humid. [ ]

4 It's wet and windy. [ ]

5 It's rainy and freezing. [ ]

Families

1 Complete the sentences. Use the words in the list.

wife | granddad | father | cousin | mother
husband | sister | grandma | aunt | uncle

0 My mother is my father's _____*wife*_____ .

1 My _____ is my mother's mother.

2 My _____ is my aunt's child.

3 My uncle is my aunt's _____ .

4 My aunt is my cousin's _____ .

5 My aunt is my father's _____ .

6 My _____ is my grandmother's husband.

7 My _____ is my cousin's father.

8 My _____ is my mother's husband.

9 My mother's sister is my _____ .

2 🔊02 **Listen and complete the table.**

	Relation to Zoë	Age	Nationality	Job
Jess				*student*
Tom				
Karen				

3 **Choose three people from your family. Write one or two sentences about each one.**

My aunt's name is Laura. She's from Brasilia.
She's 34 and she's a businesswoman.

SUMMING UP

1 (Circle) **the correct words.**

A Hey, what ⁰*you are* / *are you* doing?

B I'm writing an email to my ¹*cousin* / *sister* Gabriel in Buenos Aires.

A In Buenos Aires? What ²*does he do* / *is he doing* there? Is he there on holiday?

B Yes. His mother – my ³*aunt* / *uncle* – married an Argentinian man. They're there on holiday, visiting the family.

A That's nice. Is the weather good there right now?

B Yes, Gabriel said it was ⁴*hot and sunny* / *freezing*.

A Hot? But it's January!

B In Argentina, January is summer, remember?

A Oh, right. Listen. ⁵*Are you* / *Do you* like watching films on TV?

B Yes, why?

A There's a great film on this evening. Come and watch it with us.

B OK, thanks. But I'll finish my email first!

B EXPERIENCES
Meeting people (tense revision)

1 **Match the pictures and the sentences.**

1 She's met lots of famous people. ☐

2 She met the president last night. ☐

3 She was having dinner with the president when her phone rang. ☐

2 **Complete the sentences. Use *he* and the verb *eat* in the tenses in brackets.**

0 ___*He ate*___ a really good curry last night.
(past simple positive)

1 _____ any breakfast this morning.
(past simple negative)

2 **A** _____ all his vegetables?
(past simple question)

B _____ (negative short answer)

3 _____ when I phoned him.
(past continuous statement)

4 **A** _____ Japanese food?
(present perfect question with *ever*)

B _____ (positive short answer)

3 **Complete the sentences. Use the correct forms of the verbs.**

A Have you ever ⁰___*been*___ (be) late for a concert?

B Yes. I ¹_____ (be) late for a big concert last year. It was Florence and the Machine.

A What ²_____ (happen)?

B Well, I ³_____ (miss) my train. So I ⁴_____ (get) to the concert hall at 9 o'clock, not 8 o'clock.

A ⁵_____ you _____ (see) the show?

B Yes. The concert ⁶_____ (start) at 8.45, so of course, when I ⁷_____ (go) in the band ⁸_____ (play). But I ⁹_____ (see) about 75 per cent of the show. And it's the best concert I ¹⁰_____ ever _____ (see)!

Irregular past participles

1 **Write the past participles of the verbs.**

1 think _____
2 ride _____
3 have _____
4 drink _____
5 read _____

6 go _____
7 see _____
8 win _____
9 eat _____
10 wear _____

5

2 Complete the sentences. Use the verbs from Exercise 1.

0 Someone has *drunk* my orange juice!

1 This book's great. I've _____ it five times.

2 I haven't _____ the film yet. Is it good?

3 I love motorbikes, but I've never _____ one.

4 I've got a suit, but I've never _____ it.

5 She isn't here. She's _____ to the park.

6 I've never _____ a prize.

3 Complete the sentences. Use the correct forms of the verbs.

0 No ice cream, thanks. I've *eaten* (eat) enough.

1 Oh, you're from Peru? I _____ (think) you were Spanish.

2 This book is great. Have you _____ (read) it?

3 I've _____ (lose) my keys. Have you got them?

4 We _____ (run), but we still missed the train.

5 I _____ (go) to bed late, so I'm tired today.

6 I know I've _____ (see) that man before, but I can't remember where it was.

7 I _____ (wear) this dress to the party last week.

8 We _____ (ride) 30 km on our bikes yesterday.

Losing things

1 Put the conversation in order.

	JACK	What did you lose?
	JACK	So what did you do? Did you find it?
	JACK	What?! That's not losing something – that's just a story about being untidy!
1	JACK	Have you ever lost anything really important?
	JACK	How did you find it? Where was it?
	JACK	That's terrible! How did you feel?
	DANA	My mobile phone. It wasn't expensive, but it had all my friends' numbers on it.
	DANA	Well, I got my mum's phone and I rang my number. I heard it ringing. It was somewhere in my bedroom. I looked in the wardrobe. It wasn't there. Then I looked under the bed and there it was.
	DANA	Horrible. It was like losing my whole life.
	DANA	Yes, I have.
	DANA	Yes, happily, I did.

2 Read the conversation again. Answer the questions.

0 What did Dana lose?
She lost her mobile phone.

1 How did she feel about losing it?

_____

2 Why did she feel this way?

_____

3 How did she find it?

_____

4 Where did she find it?

_____

5 What does Jack think about her story?

_____

Furniture

1 Put the words in order to make items in a house.

0 keds   *desk*

1 elvsesh   _____

2 pretac   _____

3 reshwo   _____

4 otilte   _____

5 oreokc   _____

6 foas   _____

7 rirrmo   _____

8 archmira   _____

9 bedrarow   _____

10 nustaric   _____

11 palm   _____

2 Which of the items in Exercise 1 might you find in each room? Some items might be in more than one room.

1 bedroom
wardrobe

2 living room

_____

3 kitchen

_____

4 dining room

_____

5 bathroom

_____

SUMMING UP

1 (Circle) the correct words.

A Why didn't you come to the match yesterday?

B Oh, I was busy. I [0]*painted / (was painting)* my bedroom. I still [1]*haven't finished / didn't finish*.

A Are you just changing the colour of the walls?

B No, I've got some new things, too. Last weekend I [2]*bought / have bought* a new desk and some [3]*shelves / curtains* for the window. I want to get a new lamp, too. But I [4]*didn't see / haven't seen* anything I like yet.

A There's a new shop in town. I saw it when we [5]*shopped / were shopping*. They've got nice lamps.

B Thanks. I'll go and have a look.

C EATING AND DRINKING
Buying and talking about food

1 Complete the questions using the words in the list.

~~got any~~ | everything | How many | else
How much | Would you like | help you

0 Have you _got any_ of those Spanish oranges?

1 Is that _____?

2 Can I _____?

3 _____ would you like?

4 _____ some of those?

5 Anything _____?

6 _____ is that?

2 🔊 03 Complete the conversation with the phrases from Exercise 1. Then listen and check.

ASSISTANT Good afternoon. [0] _Can I help you?_

CUSTOMER Yes, I'd like some apples, please.

ASSISTANT [1] _____

CUSTOMER Six big ones, please.

ASSISTANT OK, [2] _____

CUSTOMER Yes. [3] _____

ASSISTANT I'm afraid we haven't got any. We've got some really nice ones from South Africa. [4] _____

CUSTOMER Sure. I'll have three.

ASSISTANT [5] _____

CUSTOMER Yes, it is. [6] _____

ASSISTANT That's £3.80 altogether.

CUSTOMER Here you are.

ASSISTANT And £1.20 change. Thanks!

3 (Circle) the correct words.

0 I think there are (some) / *any* eggs in the fridge.

1 I don't want *some / any* cake, thanks.

2 I'd like 500 grams of cheese and *some / any* ham, please.

3 I'm sorry. There isn't *some / any* pizza left.

4 I haven't got *some / any* butter in my sandwich.

5 This soup is really good. Try *some / any*.

In a restaurant

1 Put the words in order to make sentences. Write W (waiter) or C (customer).

0 I / the / please / can / menu, / see   [C]
   Can I see the menu, please ?

1 ready / you / are / order / to   [ ]
   _____ ?

2 OK / everything / is   [ ]
   _____ ?

3 much / too / chicken / the / salt / on / there's   [ ]
   _____ .

4 can / please / have / bill, / the / we   [ ]
   _____ ?

5 a / please / four, / for / table   [ ]
   _____ .

2 Complete the sentences with *much* or *many*.

0 There are too _many_ small children in this restaurant.

1 There is too _____ salt in this soup.

2 There are too _____ things on the menu.

3 There's too _____ noise in here.

4 There are too _____ chairs at this table.

5 That's too _____ money.

3 Match the sentences from Exercise 2 with the replies.

a I agree. It's disgusting.   [ ]

b I'll take some away. How many do you need?   [ ]

c Yes, I really don't know what to choose.   [ ]

d That's no problem. It's your birthday and I want you to choose whatever you want.   [ ]

e Well, it is a family restaurant.   [O]

f Yes, let's go somewhere quieter.   [ ]

Shops / Things you have to do

1 Look at the pictures. Write the shops.

chemist's

**2 ⊙Circle the correct words. Then match the
sentences with the pictures from Exercise 1.**

a You *have to / don't have to* put a stamp on it. ☐ 3

b You *have to / don't have to* wait here. ☐

c You *have to / don't have to* try clothes on
over there. ☐

d You *have to / don't have to* keep medicines
away from children. ☐

**3 What do these customer notices mean?
Write sentences using *have to* or *don't have to*.**

0 'Buy now, pay later.'
*You can have the item now, but you don't have
to pay for it yet.*

1 'Please ask assistant before trying on clothes.'

2 'Cash only – no credit or debit cards accepted.'

3 'We can deliver your shopping to your home.'

SUMMING UP

**1 Complete the conversations. Write one word in
each space.**

0 A Why are you going to the _newsagent's_ ?
   B To buy a magazine.

1 A My pen's broken.
   B Well, you don't _____ to buy a new one.
      You can use mine.

2 A I'd like _____ olives, please. 250 grams.
   B OK, here you are. Anything _____ ?

3 A What's the matter?
   B I don't feel well. I've eaten too _____ food.

D LOOKING AHEAD
Plans and arrangements

1 Look at Mia's diary. Write her plans for the day.

TODAY

8 am – meet Liam for breakfast

10 am – walk in park with Olivia

1 pm – lunch with Mum and Dad

3 pm – dentist

6 pm – train to Manchester

9 pm – film with Paula

0 At 8 am *she's meeting Liam for breakfast.*

1 After that _____

2 At 1 pm _____

3 Two hours later _____

4 At 6 pm _____

5 Finally, at 9 pm _____

**2 Read the sentences and write *I* (intention) or
A (arrangement).**

0 We're having a coffee too. ☐ A

1 I'm going to read during the journey. ☐

2 I'm going to have yogurt and cereal. ☐

3 We're meeting at the new restaurant in town. ☐

4 I'm just having a check-up – I hope. ☐

5 We're seeing Jennifer Lawrence's latest
film – I can't wait. ☐

**3 Write about four arrangements you've got for
this week.**

_____
_____
_____

Sports and sport verbs

1 ⊙Circle the correct words.

0 Do you want to *go / do / ⊙play* football later?

1 We *went / did / played* skiing last weekend.

2 My friend Alex *goes / does / plays* rock climbing
every weekend.

3 We have to *go / do / play* gymnastics on Fridays.

4 I hate tennis. I never want to *go / do / play* it again!

5 Mum *goes / does / plays* running every morning.

6 We go to the sports ground on Sundays to *go / do
/ play* some athletics.

7 Let's go to the gym. We can *go / do / play* karate.

Travel and plans

1   Match the sentence halves.

0   We arrived late at the railway station
     and missed ☐ *f*

1   It was late and we were tired, so we took ☐

2   My mum's car is at the garage, so I rode ☐

3   We left the cinema at 10 pm and caught ☐

4   Last year we flew ☐

5   He really wanted to get home, so he drove ☐

a   my bike to school today.

b   the last bus home.

c   to Colombia for our holidays.

d   a taxi home from the airport.

e   all night.

f   the train by three minutes.

2   Write five sentences about the transport you use in your life.

0   *When we go on holiday, we usually fly.*

1   _____

2   _____

3   _____

4   _____

5   _____

3   ◀))04   Listen to the conversation. Answer the questions.

0   Where is Martha going for her holiday?
     She's going to Italy.

1   How long is she going for?
     _____

2   How is she getting there?
     _____

3   When is she leaving?
     _____

4   What does she need to buy in town?
     _____

5   What's her problem?
     _____

4   ◀))04   Complete the conversation with the words in the list. Then listen again and check.

~~going to have~~ | going to be | going to buy
taking | taxi | driving | leaving | flying
going to spend | train

BEN   Are you 0 *going to have* a holiday
           this year?

MARTHA Yes. We're 1_____ two weeks
           in Italy.

BEN   Lucky you. Are you 2_____?

MARTHA No, we're not. We're 3_____
           the train. It's 4_____ a real
           adventure.

BEN   That sounds really exciting.

MARTHA Yes, in fact, we're 5_____ next
           Monday. We're taking a 6_____
           to the station and then it's the
           7_____ all the way to Genoa.

BEN   Are you ready to go?

MARTHA Almost. I'm 8_____ to town
           tomorrow to do a few last-minute things.

BEN   Like what?

MARTHA Well, I'm 9_____ some more
           summer clothes and then I need to go to
           the post office.

BEN   The post office? Why?

MARTHA I've got to get a new passport.

BEN   A passport! You can't just get a passport
           that quickly.

MARTHA Oh. Can't you?

SUMMING UP

1   Complete the email. Write one word in each space.

Hi Jack,

You know our school volleyball team won the local championship last year, right? Well, this month we're playing teams from other cities in the UK.

Next Saturday, we're 0 *playing* against a team in Scotland. It's a long way, so we aren't 1_____ the train – we're 2_____ there! I've never been on a plane before, so I'm really excited.

I'm going to stay in Scotland until Monday. On Sunday, I hope to 3_____ some rock climbing. There are some great places for it up there. My friend Steve wants to 4_____ skiing, but I don't think there's enough snow.

I'll write when we come back and tell you all about it.
Best,
Sandy

1 AMAZING PEOPLE

GRAMMAR

Present perfect with *just*, *already* and *yet* SB p.14

1 ★☆☆ **Complete the sentences with *just*, *already* or *yet*.**

My little sister is really smart.

1 She's _____ learned to walk. She took her first steps last week.

2 She hasn't learned to read _____ , but she likes the pictures.

3 She's _____ learned to count from one to five and she's only one year old!

2 ★★☆ **Look at Jake's to-do list for tidying his bedroom. Write sentences using *already* and *yet*.**

- tidy desk ✓
- put CDs on shelf ✗
- pick up towels and put them in bathroom ✗
- make bed ✓
- take bin downstairs ✗
- hang up clothes ✓

Jake has *already tidied his desk.*

_____

_____

Jake hasn't _____

_____

_____

3 ★★★ **Look at the pictures. What has just happened? Write sentences using the verbs in A and the words in B.**

A	B
~~wake~~	~~up~~
fall	a goal
have	an accident
score	over
start	the trophy
win	to rain

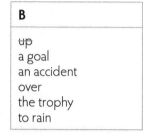

0 He *has just woken up.*

1 They _____

2 They _____

3 She _____

4 She _____

5 It _____

Present perfect vs. past simple `SB p.17`

4 ★☆☆ **Match the questions and answers.**

0	b	Have you played volleyball?
1	☐	Where did you play?
2	☐	Did you enjoy it?
3	☐	Were you good at it?
4	☐	Has your team won anything?
5	☐	Has your team been to different countries?

a No, I wasn't.

b Yes, I have.

c Yes, we've already won three competitions.

d At school.

e No, we haven't – not yet.

f No, not very much.

5 ★★☆ **Complete the conversation. Use the present perfect or past simple and the information in brackets.**

It's Sunday afternoon.

PETER Mum, I'm bored. What can I do?

MUM (finish your homework?)

⁰ *Have you finished your homework?*

PETER (last night)
Yes, I finished it all last night.

MUM (tidy your room?)

1 _____

PETER (yesterday)

2 _____

MUM (take the dog out?)

3 _____

PETER (before lunch)

4 _____

MUM (wash your bike?)

5 _____

PETER (on Friday)

6 _____

MUM (phone Jim?)

7 _____

PETER (this morning / no answer)

8 _____

MUM (watch your new DVD?)

9 _____

PETER (last night)

10 _____

MUM Well, I don't know. What about helping me with the washing up?

PETER Erm … maybe not!

6 ★★★ **Complete the text. Use the present perfect or past simple of the verbs in the list. You can use some verbs more than once.**

do | have | work | not finish | not learn
stop | be | buy | live | get | look

My grandmother is 65 and ⁰*has done* a lot of things in her life. She ¹_____ born in the country and ²_____ on a small farm until she was sixteen. She ³_____ in many different places, but she always says the farm ⁴_____ the best place of all. She ⁵_____ school because she started working when she was fifteen. She ⁶_____ many different jobs in her life – she ⁷_____ a children's nurse, a dressmaker and a shop assistant among other things. She ⁸_____ in a very expensive shop in London for several years. She ⁹_____ working after she ¹⁰_____ married. She ¹¹_____ five children and she ¹²_____ after the house. Grandma loves new things. She ¹³_____ just _____ a laptop, but she ¹⁴_____ how to send emails yet. I'm going to her house to help her now.

GET IT RIGHT! 👁

Present perfect with *just*, *already* and *yet*

Learners often make word order errors with *just*, *already* and *yet*.

✓ I **have just** finished my homework.

✗ I ~~just have~~ finished my homework.

✓ He has not **passed his exam yet**.

✗ He has not ~~passed yet his exam~~.

✓ We **have already finished** our project.

✗ We ~~already have finished~~ our project.

Correct the following sentences.

0 I already have finished my application.
   I have already finished my application.

1 My brother has yet not had a summer job.
   _____

2 I already have learned to drive.
   _____

3 My friends and I have been just on holiday.
   _____

4 Have you yet bought your mum a birthday present?
   _____

5 The singer has released already five albums.
   _____

6 I just have finished writing my blog for this week.
   _____

VOCABULARY

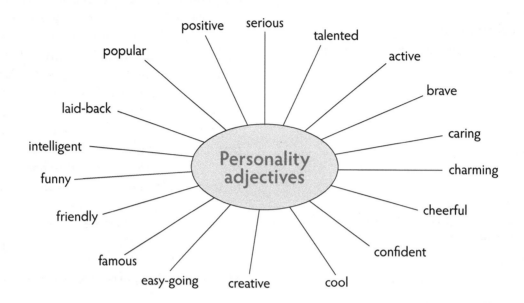

Collocations

do a degree / an interview
make a cake / friends
miss the bus / your family
sign a contract / an autograph
win a competition / a prize
write a novel / a song

just

It was **just** a joke.
Tom's **just** arrived.
The book was **just** fantastic!

Key words in context

admire	She never gives up, and I **admire** her for that.
attract	The Eiffel Tower **attracts** thousands of visitors every year.
complain	The food was horrible, so we decided to **complain** to the waiter.
decorate	I'm going to **decorate** my bedroom with pictures and posters.
genius	He wrote music when he was only five years old! He was a **genius**.
hero	She helped the country to become independent, and now she's a national **hero**.
organise	I'm going to **organise** a party for him.
original	No one else paints like him – he has very **original** ideas.
poem	I gave her a book of **poems** for her birthday.
round of applause	The audience loved the music, and they gave the musicians a big **round of applause** at the end.

Personality adjectives `SB p.12`

1 ★★☆ (Circle) the correct option: A, B or C.

0	An active person	A loves theatre.	(B) is always doing something.	C sleeps a lot.
1	A brave person	A takes risks when it's necessary.	B is often angry.	C doesn't like talking.
2	A creative person	A often makes mistakes.	B has original ideas.	C works very hard.
3	A charming person	A is very good-looking.	B has a lot of money.	C is easy to talk to.
4	A cheerful person	A often feels sad.	B enjoys life.	C often gets angry.
5	A laid-back person	A is very relaxed.	B can't wake up in the morning.	C never goes out.
6	A confident person	A doesn't work hard.	B believes in him-/herself.	C will keep a secret.
7	A positive person	A sees the good in everything.	B is frightened of the future.	C is often bored.
8	A talented person	A has got a lot of money.	B isn't good at sports.	C is good at something.

2 ★★☆ Read the text. Complete the adjectives. The first and last letters are given.

My ideal friend is very ^{0}_active_ – that's important because I play a lot of sports and I want him to play basketball in my team. He's ^{1}l_____-_____k and knows how to have fun, so he's a good person to hang out with. I need a friend who's really ^{2}t_____d with computers, because I'm not good at IT and he could help me. Maybe it would be good if he was ^{3}c_____g too – I'm not very ^{4}c_____t, so he can help me talk to girls! (I know – I need to be more ^{5}p_____e, right?)

3 ★★★ Write one or two sentences about people you know (friends or family). Use adjectives from Exercises 1 and 2.

_____

_____

_____

_____

Collocations `SB p.17`

4 ★☆☆ Complete the text with the words in the list.

~~won~~ | write | do | signed | missed | have

Last year, Jason's band were on TV – they ^{0} _won_ a talent show. Jason was a bit unhappy because his mum ^{1}_____ the show (she was ill). But the band members are very excited because they've just^2_____ a contract with a record company.

The band members are talented musicians – they ^{3}_____ all their own songs. They're hoping to ^{4}_____ a lot of success on the music scene. Tomorrow morning, Jason is going to ^{5}_____ an interview on TV.

5 ★★☆ Complete the text. Use the correct forms of the verbs in A and the words in B.

A ~~have~~ make (x2) sign do

B ~~a party~~ albums a degree a cake his autograph

The members of Jason's band ^{0} _are having a party_ to celebrate. Jason's mum has ^{1}_____ . Some of the band's friends are asking Jason to ^{2}_____ on their T-shirts. Cherie, the singer, is still planning to ^{3}_____ in music at university next year, but says she can still ^{4}_____ with the band.

WordWise `SB p.19`
Phrases with *just*

6 ★★☆ Tick (✓) the five sentences that can be completed by adding *just*.

0	I've … cleaned the floor.	✓
1	That horror film, *The Blob,* is … terrifying.	☐
2	He can't tell you if you don't … ask.	☐
3	This dress is almost … perfect.	☐
4	The flower show was … amazing.	☐
5	He's … a child, but he's a talented artist.	☐
6	No problem, it was … a thought.	☐
7	Gemma has … phoned. She's on her way.	☐

7 ★★☆ Match the sentences in Exercise 6 with the meanings of *just*.

1	a short time ago	0 ☐
2	only	☐ ☐
3	really	☐ ☐

READING

1 REMEMBER AND CHECK **Match the people with the statements. Then check your answers in the online survey on page 13 of the Student's Book.**

1 Bia's mum

2 Mr Donaldson

3 Alex's grandmother, Gwen

4 Uncle Jack

☐ a spends a lot of time away from home.

☐ b has just done a parachute jump for charity.

☐ c is very laid-back.

☐ d devotes all his time to his family.

☐ e is a wildlife photographer.

☐ f is a seriously talented guitarist.

☐ g has three children.

☐ h has been on TV.

☐ i is 78 years old.

☐ j never complains.

☐ k is a music teacher.

☐ l thinks life is for living.

2 **Read the article. Tick (✓) four jobs that it mentions.**

1 comedian ☐

2 film star ☐

3 songwriter ☐

4 novelist ☐

5 singer ☐

6 translator ☐

3 **Read the article again. Mark the sentences T (true) or F (false).**

0 Joseph Conrad started to learn English when he was twenty. | F |

1 Conrad spoke English like an English person. ☐

2 Conrad's novels aren't very good. ☐

3 Victor Borge was a talented musician as a child. ☐

4 Borge learned English at school. ☐

5 Borge was a comedian on TV in the USA. ☐

6 ABBA were from Switzerland. ☐

4 **Do you know any other people who do things incredibly well in a language that isn't their first language? Who?**

AMAZING LEARNERS OF ENGLISH

We all know that a lot of people – and I mean a *lot* of people – learn another language and get really good at it. I'm not including bilingual people whose parents speak different languages to them from when they're born. (They're lucky – they don't even have to try, right?) No, I mean people who learn at school or even later and then get so good at their second language that they become famous in it.

Here's an example: a Polish man called Joseph Conrad. Well, his 'real' name was Józef Teodor Konrad Korzeniowski and he was born in 1857. When he was in his twenties, he became a sailor and started to learn English. Then he went to live in England. He stayed there for the rest of his life and he always spoke English with an accent. So what? Well, he changed his name to Joseph Conrad and he wrote novels in English. He wrote about twenty novels that a lot of people think are some of the greatest novels in English.

Another example? OK. Børge Rosenbaum was born in Denmark in 1909. He was an extremely good pianist – he gave his first concert when he was just eight years old! Later, he started to tell jokes when he played the piano and he became a piano-playing comedian – in Danish, of course. Then, when the Second World War started, he managed to escape from Denmark and he went to the USA. He was 31, he had $20 in his pocket and he spoke no English at all. So, to learn English, he watched films and went to watch American comedians. Then he changed his name to Victor Borge, started doing his own comedy acts and became a famous TV comedian – making jokes in his second language!

Then perhaps you can add the Swedish group ABBA, who became incredibly famous writing and singing songs in English. There must be others, but I don't know any more. Do you?

DEVELOPING WRITING

A person I know well

1 Read the text that Emily wrote about her friend Patrick. Match the pictures with three of the paragraphs.

A I'm going to write about one of my friends, Patrick. We met when he moved into a house in my street three years ago.

B He's a little older than me, but I always feel like he's much older! I think that's because he's a very confident person – he's only fourteen, but he's very sure of himself. When Patrick talks to adults, he talks to them like he's an adult too. He isn't afraid to disagree with adults, for example. I've never said 'No, I don't agree' to an adult, but Patrick has! I think that's a good point about him.

C Another good point is that he's very honest. If he doesn't like something, he says so. He never says 'Oh yes, it's great', just to be the same as everyone else. In fact, this is why some people at school don't like him very much, I think.

D Does he have bad points? Yes! He's forgetful. I remember a few times when he promised to do something, and he just forgot! Once he promised to come to my house and help me with something. He didn't come, so I phoned him. Like I said, he's honest, so he said, 'Oh, no. I forgot. I'll come right now.' And he did. He arrived with a big smile, saying, 'I'm awful, aren't I? I always forget. Sorry.' I couldn't be angry with him!

E I hope we're going to be friends for a long time.

2 How many good things and how many bad things does Emily write about?

_____

_____

3 Which adjectives describe Patrick? Tick (✓) three.

1	polite ☐	4	confident ☐
2	honest ☐	5	forgetful ☐
3	intelligent ☐	6	talented ☐

4 Look at the three boxes you ticked in Exercise 3. What examples does Emily give to show that these adjectives describe Patrick?

1 _____

_____

2 _____

_____

3 _____

_____

5 Read the text again. Match the paragraphs A–E with the topics.

0 A not-so-good thing about Patrick   [D]

1 First good thing about Patrick   ☐

2 Closing   ☐

3 Who the person is   ☐

4 Another good thing about Patrick   ☐

6 Write about someone you know, perhaps a friend or a family member (150–200 words).

● Think about the person you're going to write about. How will you introduce them to your reader?

● What are the good things and what are the not-so-good things about them? In what order will you write about them?

● What adjectives are you going to use? What examples can you use to show what you mean by each adjective?

● How will you close your writing?

LISTENING

1 🔊05 **Listen to the conversation. Circle the correct words.**

1 They're discussing *last weekend / going to a film / their parents*.
2 They both like *an actor / a film / London*.

2 🔊05 **Listen again. Mark the sentences T (true) or F (false).**

0 Maggie thinks last weekend was exciting. | T |

1 A film premiere is the first time a new film is shown. ☐

2 Maggie wants to go the premiere of Liam Hemsworth's new film. ☐

3 Maggie thinks her parents will be happy for her to go. ☐

4 Jason has an aunt and uncle who live in London. ☐

5 Jason doesn't want to go to the film with Maggie. ☐

6 Jason doesn't like Liam Hemsworth. ☐

7 Jason and Maggie are going to talk to Maggie's parents. ☐

3 🔊05 **Listen again. Complete the conversations.**

1 MAGGIE Well, you know that Liam Hemsworth is my absolute film hero?

JASON Yes, ⁰ *of course I know* that.
So ¹_____?

2 MAGGIE Well, I'm going to the premiere!

JASON Oh, that's a ²_____!

MAGGIE Oh? Do you really think so?

JASON Yes, you ³_____ do it. You've always wanted to meet him.

3 MAGGIE Wow, that's great! Thank you. I'm just worried that my parents …
⁴_____, they won't like the idea.

JASON I know what you mean. But, hey, you know what? You've got to
⁵_____!

Pronunciation

Sentence stress

Go to page 118. 🔊

DIALOGUE

1 **Put the conversations in the correct order.**

CONVERSATION 1

☐ A We can put a football match together between our street and Nelson Street.

|1| A I've got an idea for the weekend.

☐ A Let's speak to some people about it now.

☐ B I'll come with you. We can do it together.

☐ B A football match? That's a great idea.

☐ B Yeah? What is it?

CONVERSATION 2

☐ A Thanks, but I'm not sure if we can do everything before Saturday.

|1| A Julie, why don't we have a party?

☐ A I don't know. Can people come on Sunday?

☐ A Well, the next day's Monday – that's why. You know, homework to do, that sort of thing.

☐ B A party? Wow, yes! I'll help you if you want. Let's have it this weekend.

☐ B OK, so forget Saturday. But you should definitely do it. It could be Sunday.

☐ B Oh, don't worry about homework, Sue. Come on! You've got to make this happen!

☐ B Yes, I think they can. Why not?

PHRASES FOR FLUENCY `SB p.19`

1 **Put the words in order to make expressions.**

0 what / know *Know what?*

1 sure / you / are / ? _____

2 it / let's / face _____

3 that / and / that's _____

4 so / don't / think / I _____

5 of / sort / thing / that _____

2 **Complete the conversations with the expressions in Exercise 1.**

0 A Hurry up. The film starts at 8.30.
B *Are you sure?* I heard it starts at 9.00.

1 A How did the tennis match go?
B I lost. _____, I'm awful at tennis!

2 A So what did you do over the weekend?
B Not much – read, watched TV, _____.

3 A Oh, Dad! Can I please watch *The Voice*?
B No, you can't. I said no TV _____.

4 A I know it's raining, but let's go for a walk.
B _____? I'm staying right here!

5 A This song's just fantastic.
B Well, _____. It's terrible.

16

Writing part 1

1 For each question, complete the second sentence so that it means the same as the first. Use no more than three words.

0 Tennis is my hobby.

I really like _playing_ tennis.

1 There are more than 100 people in my Facebook friends list.

I've _____ than 100 friends on Facebook.

2 Tom is a friend of my brother's.

Tom _____ friend.

3 I've just spoken to my mum on the phone.

I _____ my mum on the phone a few minutes ago.

4 Nigel's only two, but he can ride a bike.

Nigel has _____ to ride a bike and he's only two.

5 I'm always really interested when my granddad tells stories of the past.

My granddad's stories of the past are always _____ .

Exam guide: sentence transformations

In this section there are five questions about a certain topic. Each question contains a pair of sentences. The first sentence is complete. The second sentence says the same thing as the first sentence, but some words are missing. You have to write between one and three words to complete the gap in the second sentence.

- This question tests how well you know grammar. When you read through each pair of sentences, see if you can identify what the grammatical area is. This will help you focus on the answer. Common areas include *for* vs. *since*, comparatives and superlatives, *too* vs. *enough*, adverbs and adjectives and their opposites, *there is* vs. *have got*, etc.

- When you've written in your answer, read it 'out loud' in your head. Does it sound right? If not, rethink your answer.

- Does your answer mean exactly the same as the first sentence?

- Sometimes there may be more than one answer. Don't worry about this. Write in the answer you feel more confident about.

- Be careful with your spelling – you'll get no marks if you misspell a word.

- Make sure you write no more than three words or you'll get no points for the question, even if your answer completes the sentence correctly.

---

2 For each question, complete the second sentence so that it means the same as the first. Use no more than three words.

0 Tennis is my hobby.

I really like _playing_ tennis.

1 This is my first time on a plane.

I've _____ on a plane before.

2 Buy your ticket today. It will be more expensive tomorrow.

If you _____ your ticket today, it will be more expensive tomorrow.

3 I've got a flight to Milan in the morning.

I'm _____ to Milan in the morning.

4 No car is more expensive than this one.

This is _____ car in the world.

5 You can buy your ticket on the train.

You _____ buy your ticket before you get on the train.

2 | THE WAYS WE LEARN

GRAMMAR

Present perfect with *for* and *since* SB p.22

1 ★☆☆ **Complete the sentences with *for* or *since* and a number where necessary.**

0 Matthew has worked as a computer games tester _*for*_ three years.

1 I've lived in this house _____ 2011.

2 We've had our pet rabbit _____ only six weeks.

3 Lauren has played the guitar in the band _____ she was 16 years old.

4 This tree has been here _____ more than 200 years!

5 I've written poems _____ I was ten years old.

6 Charlotte has been in the football team _____ 2013, so she has been a footballer _____ _____ years.

7 Joshua has played tennis _____ he was four years old. He was born in 2010, so he has played tennis _____ _____ years.

2 ★★☆ **Write sentences. Use the positive and negative form of the present perfect and *for* or *since*.**

0 Thomas / not see / grandfather / two months
   Thomas hasn't seen his grandfather for two months.

1 Steve and Jane / be / singers / five years
   _____

2 Sophie / not play / football / she broke her leg
   _____

3 Harry / not write / on his blog / a long time
   _____

4 Sam / not go / to the dentist / a year
   _____

5 George and I / be / friends / we were kids
   _____

6 They / not see / a good film / more than a month
   _____

7 We / not go / on holiday / two years
   _____

3 ★★☆ **Jessie wants to ask her friends some questions for a school project. Complete them with the present perfect form of the verbs.**

1 How long _*have you lived*_ (live) in your house?

2 What is your best friend's name? How long _____ (know) him/her?

3 How long _____ (be) at this school?

4 What's your favourite possession? How long _____ (have) it?

4 ★★★ **Look at the table and write answers to Jessie's questions. Use the present perfect and *for* or *since*.**

	Emily	Jack	Dan
1	ten years	2010	three months
2	Sarah, 2009	Harry, 2012	Jim, a long time
3	five years	2012	September
4	bike, six months	dog, two years	laptop, May

1 Emily *has lived in her house for ten years.*

2 _____

3 _____

4 _____

1 Jack _____

2 _____

3 _____

4 _____

1 Dan _____

2 _____

3 _____

4 _____

5 ★★★ **Answer the questions in Exercise 3 for you.**

1 _____

2 _____

3 _____

4 _____

a, an, the or no article SB p.25

6 ★ ☆ ☆ (Circle) the correct words.

Yesterday I went to ^{0}(*the*)/ *an* park. I go there a lot, so I know ^{1}*a* / *the* park very well. I sat on ^{2}*a* / *the* grass and started to read my book. Then lots of ^{3}*the* / – things started to happen.

You can do lots of things in the park, but ^{4}*the* / – bicycles aren't allowed. There was ^{5}*a* / *the* boy on ^{6}*a* / *the* bicycle who was riding on the path. ^{7}– / *The* park keeper started to run after ^{8}*a* / *the* boy on the bike, but she couldn't catch him.

There were three small boys playing ^{9}– / *the* football in the park too, and when one of them kicked ^{10}*a* / *the* ball, it hit ^{11}*a* / *the* boy on the bicycle and he fell off his bike. So the park keeper got him! I think this is ^{12}*an* / *the* example of ^{13}– / *the* really bad luck!

7 ★★ ☆ Complete the text with *a, an, the* or – (no article).

People have kept ^{0}____ — ____ cats as pets for thousands of years. Cats are ^{1}_____ good example of how ^{2}_____ animal can help ^{3}_____ people, by catching ^{4}_____ rats and ^{5}_____ mice, for example. This is probably ^{6}_____ most important reason ancient people had ^{7}_____ cats. These days, many people have a cat at home, but they only keep it for ^{8}_____ pleasure. Sometimes the cat sits on ^{9}_____ owner's chair or knee, and the owner gets ^{10}_____ pleasant feeling when that happens.

8 ★★ ☆ Read the sentences. Tick (✓) the four that are correct.

1 I love the dogs. ☐
2 I saw a beautiful dog in the park yesterday. ☐
3 The dog in the park was bigger than mine. ☐
4 It was standing beside the very small dog. ☐
5 I think the small dog was a Chihuahua. ☐
6 I think the dogs make really good friends. ☐
7 There are many different sizes of the dogs. ☐
8 I saw a picture of the biggest dog in the world. ☐

Pronunciation

Word stress

Go to page 118.

9 ★★★ **Read Exercise 8 again. Change the four incorrect sentences so that they are correct.**

1 _____
2 _____
3 _____
4 _____

GET IT RIGHT! 👁

a(n) and no article

Learners often use *a(n)* where no article is needed, and no article where *a* is needed.

✓ I had **a** great time with my friends last Saturday.
✗ ~~I had great time with my friends last Saturday.~~

Complete the sentences with *a(n)* or – no article.

0 I've got *a* pet cat.
1 My brother works as ____ chef in a hotel.
2 Do you need to book ____ accommodation?
3 We haven't had ____ holiday for ages.
4 I am ____ student at the University of London.
5 We need ____ information about this urgently.
6 I would like to buy ____ desk and chair.

VOCABULARY

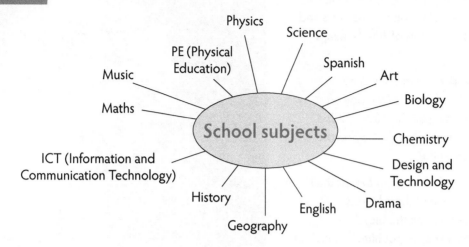

Thinking

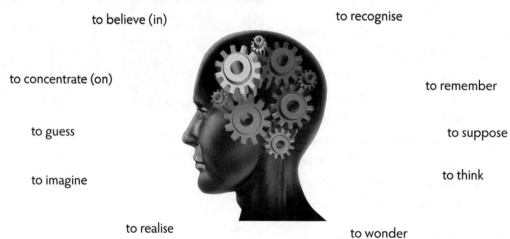

to believe (in)   to recognise

to concentrate (on)   to remember

to guess   to suppose

to imagine   to think

to realise   to wonder

Key words in context

achieve	I've worked hard all day, but I don't think I've really **achieved** anything!
away match	Our team is from London. Tomorrow they're playing an **away match** in Manchester.
encourage	His parents **encouraged** him to be a doctor, but he only wanted to be an actor.
exhausted	After working hard for twelve hours, she was **exhausted**.
motivation	He doesn't like his job. He hasn't got any **motivation** to work hard.
performance	It was his first time on the stage, and he gave a great **performance**.
planet	The nearest **planet** to Earth is Venus.
safety	**Safety** is very important in schools and that's why children aren't allowed to do anything dangerous.
strengthen	I did a lot of exercises to **strengthen** my arms.
teamwork	We all work very well together – it's great **teamwork**!
tool	Computers are an important **tool** for scientists.
warm-up	The players have a ten-minute **warm-up** before the game begins.
weight training	He does **weight training** and now he can lift 140 kilograms.
workshop	We went to a one-day **workshop** on 'How to look after your dog'.
youth club	The **youth club** in our town is a great place for teenagers to go to.

School subjects SB p.22

1 ★ ☆ ☆ **Put the letters in order to make school subjects.**

0 You probably need a piano if you're a (sciuM) teacher. _Music_

1 We often use computers in Design and (Thecloongy). _____

2 (regGyhoap) teachers don't need maps now that there's Google Earth. _____

3 We have our (stiChryme) lessons in one of the science labs. _____

4 Our Spanish teacher comes from Madrid. She never speaks (shEling) in class. _____

5 A calculator can be useful in a (thaMs) class. _____

6 I really enjoy (troyisH) lessons when they're about people, not just dates. _____

7 Our (amarD) teacher has been on TV and acted in a film! _____

2 ★★ ☆ **Look at the photos. Write the subjects.**

0 _Maths_ 1 _____

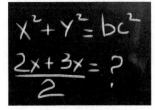

2 _____ 3 _____

4 _____ 5 _____

6 _____ 7 _____

Thinking SB p.25

3 ★ ☆ ☆ **Find the ten words about thinking.**

W	R	U	O	R	T	G	K	O	B	R
C	O	N	C	E	N	T	R	A	T	E
S	G	F	G	M	I	K	E	E	Y	B
G	T	E	U	E	E	B	A	S	E	T
I	H	G	E	M	I	H	L	I	H	I
M	I	N	S	B	E	L	I	E	V	E
A	N	S	S	E	L	V	S	Y	K	E
G	K	G	L	R	T	E	E	N	Q	L
I	F	V	U	J	X	O	L	O	K	E
N	S	U	P	P	O	S	E	G	F	L
E	U	O	M	B	W	O	N	D	E	R
P	R	E	C	O	G	N	I	S	E	C

4 ★★ ☆ **Complete the text with the words in Exercise 3.**

Do you [0]b_elieve_____ in the idea of morning people and night people? I do. I've always found it difficult to [1]c_____ in the morning. I can never [2]r_____ anything when we have a test in the morning.

I [3]w_____ why schools don't start in the evening. I [4]t_____ night people would love that. Can you [5]i_____ starting school at 8 pm? Great! We could sleep all day! But I [6]s_____ morning people would hate studying at night.

You can always [7]r_____ morning people – they're so cheerful in the mornings and don't seem to [8]r_____ that night people don't want to chat! So, am I a morning person or a night person? You can [9]g_____, can't you?

5 ★★ ☆ **Read and answer the questions.**

1 Do you believe everything you read in magazines?

_____

2 What kind of thing(s) do you remember easily?

_____

3 What time of day do you concentrate best?

_____

4 What do you imagine you will be in the future?

_____

READING

1 REMEMBER AND CHECK (Circle) the correct words. Then check your answers in the article on page 21 of the Student's Book.

0 Tinkering School has a (summer) / winter programme for kids.

1 At the school, kids learn life skills by *writing texts / building things* together.

2 Some children once built a bridge using *trees / shopping bags*.

3 Kids at the school don't suffer serious injuries because *there are health and safety regulations / they can't use knives or hammers*.

4 The 'real' school – Brightworks – has got *between six and 13 / only 20* students.

5 Most newspaper articles about Brightworks have been *critical / positive*.

6 Some people think the kids at Brightworks don't *learn / play* enough.

7 Since she started at the school, Tina Cooper *hasn't had to work hard / has never been bored*.

2 Read about Sunaina's first day at a new school in a new country. Answer the questions.

0 How did she feel about the school at the end of the first day?

She couldn't wait to leave.

1 What things made her feel bad?

_____

2 What surprised her most about the school?

_____

3 How does she feel about the school now?

_____

4 What has she learned from being at this school?

_____

3 Read the text again. Match these phrases with the correct places (A–H).

0	at the same time	B
1	but I sat by myself	☐
2	missing my mum and dad	☐
3	but that wasn't possible	☐
4	took a deep breath and	☐
5	to the class	☐
6	all kinds of	☐
7	get to know me	☐

Sunaina's family left India and moved to the USA when she was 13. She had to start a new school ...

I remember it really well. My parents drove me to the school and said goodbye to me. I (A) walked into the school.

I didn't know what to feel. I was excited and scared and a bit nervous, all (B). There were lots of other kids around. They were already in groups of friends, but none of them said hello or anything. It was a strange feeling for me, like I didn't really belong there. I wanted to be somewhere else, (C).

The first thing I had to do was register, so I went to a room in the school that had a sign saying 'Administration'. Suddenly, I felt like I was some kind of criminal. They started asking me (D) questions. Then I went off to my first class.

My first class. Wow, that was horrible. Perhaps it was because my hair or clothes were different, but everyone just looked at me in such a strange way. And just like when I arrived, no one came to talk to me. Incredibly, that's never happened: no one has ever taken the time to (E) or like me. I have friends because I made the first move to meet people.

Maybe the worst class that day, though, was Science. The teacher wasn't too bad. She introduced me (F) and showed me where to sit. But the other students? Well, they looked at me like I was a guinea pig or something they were going to use for an experiment. I hated every minute.

Then there was a break and I went to sit somewhere alone, (G). But I thought they'd want me to keep trying, so I tried to be more positive in the next class. Not so good, though. Everyone talked to other students, (H). At the end of the day, I couldn't wait to get out of there.

But, as time passed, things have got better. Now I'm doing fine and I get OK grades. I've learned lots of things – but not what the teachers teach. I've learned that I'm strong and brave. I've learned that I will succeed even if some things aren't the way I want them to be.

4 <u>Underline</u> two or three things Sunaina says that you find interesting.

5 Write two questions that you'd like to ask Sunaina. Then write what you think she'd say in reply.

0 Q *What's your favourite subject at school?*
   A *Science. I like IT too.*

1 Q _____
   A _____

2 Q _____
   A _____

DEVELOPING WRITING

An informal email

1 Read the email. Tick (✓) the things Jed talks about.

1 How he feels about his routine ☐
2 The things he likes to watch on TV ☐
3 Homework that he doesn't like to do ☐
4 A party for his birthday ☐

2 Read the phrases from the email. Match them with the words that have been left out.

0 … good to get your last email. [*b*]
1 … everything going well? ☐
2 … any chance of you coming? ☐
3 … would be great to see you here. ☐
4 … hope you can come. ☐

a I
b It was
c It
d Is
e Is there

Hi Tania,

How's it going? Good to get your last email – it was fun to read. I liked hearing about your life, your routine and stuff, so I thought I could tell you about mine.

So, what can I tell you? Most weeks are the same as other weeks, really. I guess that's true about everyone, though. Monday to Friday, well, they're school days, so that's a kind of routine. You know, get up at 7.30, go to school at 8.45, come home at 4.00 and do homework, then have dinner and go to bed. Well, that's kind of true, but, you know, lots of things make every day different, so I don't mind the routine. It's OK. Every day there are different lessons at school and different things on TV in the evening. Even the homework is different sometimes!

Anyway, I wonder how you're getting on at your new school. Everything going well? I'm sure it is – you know how to make new friends and get on with things, right?

By the way, it's my 15th birthday next month (Saturday 12th) and we're having a party. Any chance of you coming? Would be great to see you here. Hope you can come. Let me know, OK?

So, what was I saying about routine and things? Yeah, right, homework – and I've got some to do, so I'm going to stop here. But I really, really want to hear from you again soon, OK?

Take care,

Jed

---

3 Read the email again. Find these phrases.

0 What Jed says instead of *How are you?*:
   How's it going?
1 Two ways that Jed starts to talk about a different topic: _____ and _____
2 Three ways he checks that Tania is following him: _____ , _____ and _____
3 How he ends his email: _____

4 Write an email to an English-speaking friend (150–200 words). Your friend wants to know about your weekends and your routines.

- Think about how to start and finish your email.
- Think about how you can make your email friendly and chatty – for example, asking questions to check your friend is following you and/or leaving words out to sound more informal.

Writing tip: writing an informal email

- People email each other to send news, ask questions, get simple information, or just to keep in touch. Very often, people write as if they were talking to the person they're writing to.
- People often speak in short sentences, and they write in short sentences too.
- Start your email with a general *How are you?* question. Do you know other ways of saying *How are you?*
- Tell the reader straight away what you're writing about and why.
- In speaking, people use phrases like *you know* and *right?* to 'get closer' to the listener. You can do this in an informal email too.
- Find a nice, friendly way to finish your email, for example, *Take care* or *All the best* or (if you know someone very well) *Love from* … .

LISTENING

1 ◀))09 Listen to the conversations. Match each one with a photo. There is one photo that you don't need.

A ☐

B ☐

C ☐

D ☐

2 ◀))09 Listen again and answer the questions.

CONVERSATION 1

0 Where does Jimmy want to go?
   He wants to go to the toilet.

1 When does he have to come back?

_____

_____

CONVERSATION 2

2 What is the girl's project about?

_____

_____

3 Does the man let the girl take the photo?

_____

_____

CONVERSATION 3

4 Where is the boy's laptop?

_____

_____

5 When can he use Joanna's laptop?

_____

_____

DIALOGUE

1 Put the conversations in order.

1

1	GIRL	Excuse me. Is it OK if I try this shirt on?
☐	GIRL	Really? OK. Can I take a size 8 too?
☐	GIRL	OK, thanks.
☐	GIRL	I think so. This is size 6.
☐	WOMAN	Well, I think it might be too small for you.
☐	WOMAN	Of course you can. Here's a size 8. OK. Tell me when you're finished.
☐	WOMAN	Of course. Have you got the right size?

2

1	MARK	Jamie, can I ask you something?
☐	MARK	Great, thanks. Oh – another thing.
☐	MARK	Well, I forgot to charge my mobile phone. Can I take yours?
☐	MARK	I understand. Thanks anyway.
☐	MARK	Can I borrow your jeans tonight – you know, the white ones?
☐	JAMIE	Sure. What is it?
☐	JAMIE	Sorry, no way! My mobile phone goes with me everywhere.
☐	JAMIE	Yeah, go ahead. I'm not wearing them.
☐	JAMIE	Another thing? What is it?

▮▮▮ TRAIN TO THiNK ▮▮▮

Thinking about texts

1 Read the text about Sunaina on page 22 again. ⟨Circle⟩ the correct option: A, B, C or D.

1 Where *wouldn't* you find this text?

   A in a magazine   C in a newspaper

   B on a website   D in a homework book

2 What is the main purpose of the text?

   A to complain about bad schools

   B to describe a personal experience

   C to entertain the reader

   D to persuade readers not to change schools

3 What is the best title for the text?

   A What I learned in a school that I didn't like

   B My first day at school

   C Good and bad teachers

   D How to do well at a new school

Help with reading: identifying text purpose

1   Read the texts. What is the purpose of each one?

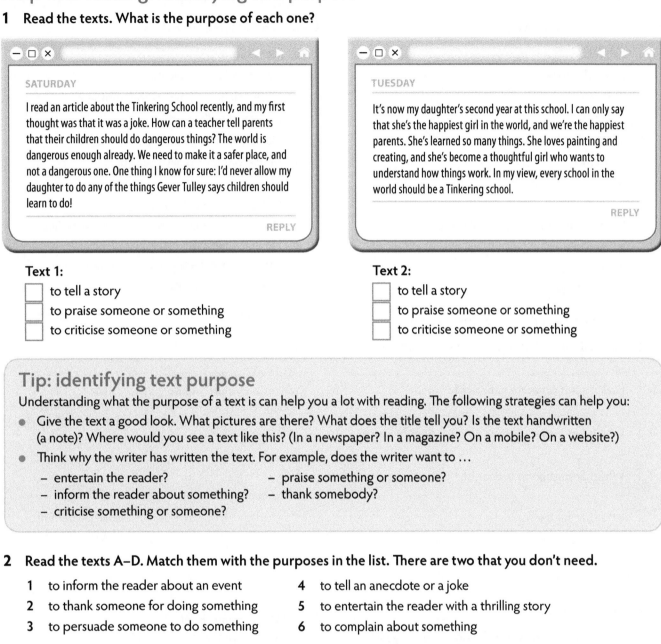

SATURDAY

I read an article about the Tinkering School recently, and my first thought was that it was a joke. How can a teacher tell parents that their children should do dangerous things? The world is dangerous enough already. We need to make it a safer place, and not a dangerous one. One thing I know for sure: I'd never allow my daughter to do any of the things Gever Tulley says children should learn to do!

REPLY

TUESDAY

It's now my daughter's second year at this school. I can only say that she's the happiest girl in the world, and we're the happiest parents. She's learned so many things. She loves painting and creating, and she's become a thoughtful girl who wants to understand how things work. In my view, every school in the world should be a Tinkering school.

REPLY

Text 1:
- ☐ to tell a story
- ☐ to praise someone or something
- ☐ to criticise someone or something

Text 2:
- ☐ to tell a story
- ☐ to praise someone or something
- ☐ to criticise someone or something

Tip: identifying text purpose

Understanding what the purpose of a text is can help you a lot with reading. The following strategies can help you:

- Give the text a good look. What pictures are there? What does the title tell you? Is the text handwritten (a note)? Where would you see a text like this? (In a newspaper? In a magazine? On a mobile? On a website?)
- Think why the writer has written the text. For example, does the writer want to …

  – entertain the reader?   – praise something or someone?
  – inform the reader about something?   – thank somebody?
  – criticise something or someone?

---

2   Read the texts A–D. Match them with the purposes in the list. There are two that you don't need.

1   to inform the reader about an event   4   to tell an anecdote or a joke
2   to thank someone for doing something   5   to entertain the reader with a thrilling story
3   to persuade someone to do something   6   to complain about something

A

The beautiful sandy beaches, the pleasantly warm seas and the friendly local people offer you the holiday of a lifetime. The crystal clear water will show you spectacular marine wildlife and will help you to forget stress and cold weather. Come to the Seychelles – you won't regret it!

Text purpose: ☐

B

I'm so grateful that you can help me with my project. I don't quite understand what to do and I'm so happy I can ask you the questions that help me understand the task.

Text purpose: ☐

C

The room was a mess. 'We've got to look at everything in here,' said the detective inspector. 'Every little bit! We know the robbers were here before they broke into the bank.' 'You won't find anything, Inspector,' a deep voice suddenly said.

Text purpose: ☐

D

Unfortunately, I have to say that we were not happy with the service we got at your hotel at all. Our room was far too small and too expensive, the meals were too small and often cold, and your waiters were very unfriendly.

Text purpose: ☐

CONSOLIDATION

LISTENING

1 🔊 10 **Listen and tick (✓) A, B or C.**

1 When did Sophie start at the school?
- A Wednesday ☐
- B Friday ☐
- C Thursday ☐

2 What is Sophie's favourite subject?
- A Science ☐
- B Art ☐
- C Spanish ☐

3 Where does Allan offer to take Sophie?
- A the library ☐
- B the school café ☐
- C the school gym ☐

2 🔊 10 **Listen again. Answer the questions.**

0 How many days has Sophie been at the school?
   _4_

1 How does it compare to her old school?
   _____

2 Who is her favourite teacher? What does he teach?
   _____

3 Why is Sophie good at Spanish?
   _____

4 Where is the library?
   _____

GRAMMAR

3 Correct the sentences.

0 I've been at Bishops High School since five years.
   I've been at Bishops High School for five years

1 It's a biggest school in our city.
   _____

2 I've yet taken some important exams.
   _____

3 But I haven't got the results already.
   _____

4 I've yet decided what I want to study at university.
   _____

5 I want to study the Spanish.
   _____

6 Bess is the my best friend at school.
   _____

VOCABULARY

4 Match the sentence halves.

0 He's so brave. [d]
1 Your brother's so laid-back. ☐
2 Have you heard Jim play the trumpet? ☐
3 My granddad's so active. ☐
4 Liam's the most positive person I know. ☐
5 Mr Harrington's really cheerful. ☐

a He's so talented.
b He's always doing something.
c He can see the good in absolutely everything.
d He isn't scared of anything.
e He's always got a big smile on his face.
f Does he ever get angry?

5 Write the subject these students are studying.

0 Oh, no! I've got paint all over my shirt. Mum's going to kill me.
   Art

1 I love acting in front of the rest of my class. It's so much fun.
   _____

2 The capital of Italy is … is … Oh, what is it? _____

3 Twelve percent of 200 is 24, isn't it?
   _____

4 I like learning about the past, but why do we have to learn all those dates?

5 I don't believe it. I've forgotten my tennis shoes. _____

6 I love doing these experiments. It's so much fun. _____

7 We're practising a song for the end-of-year concert.
   _____

DIALOGUE

6 Complete the conversation. Use the words in the list.

've decided | Let's face it | and that sort of thing. | Know what? | That's a great idea.
just | I'll help you if you want. | Are you sure? | Of course you can.

JOSH   I ⁰ *'ve decided*   to start a homework club.

CHLOE   A what?

JOSH   A homework club. It's so we can get together, discuss lessons, help each other with our homework, ¹_____

CHLOE   ²_____ Can I be in it?

JOSH   ³_____ I want you to be in it!

CHLOE   ⁴_____ I could text some people.

JOSH   OK. Who are you thinking of?

CHLOE   What about Dave?

JOSH   Dave? ⁵_____ He's way too smart. He doesn't need our help. ⁶_____ , he won't want to join.

CHLOE   Yes, but he doesn't have many friends. Maybe he'd like to join to make friends.

JOSH   ⁷_____ You might ⁸_____ be right.

CHLOE   I might.

JOSH   In fact, it's perfect. We help him make friends and he helps us with our homework. Chloë, you're a genius!

READING

7 Read the text. Mark the sentences T (True) or F (False).

0 Mrs Millington started teaching when she was 40.   **F**

1 Although she's a good teacher, she needs a bit more experience. ☐

2 Students are well behaved in her lessons. ☐

3 She really loves the subject she teaches. ☐

4 She was a TV news reporter before she became a teacher. ☐

5 She usually reported from countries with problems. ☐

6 She stopped working as a journalist when she started a family. ☐

7 Although she's a brilliant teacher, she's sometimes a bit unfriendly. ☐

My Geography teacher, Mrs Millington, is a really amazing person.

She's in her late forties, but she's only been a teacher for the last three years. You'd never know she hasn't got very much experience because she's excellent in the classroom. You'd think she's been a teacher all her professional life. Students love going to her classes. She never has any trouble from any of them because her lessons are so interesting that everyone just listens to everything she says. She's so enthusiastic about her subject and she really knows how to make her lessons interesting.

The other day we found out her secret, the reason why she's so good. Before she was a teacher she spent more thana 20 years as a war reporter for a newspaper. She spent most of her life reporting from countries all over the world, and she learned so much about these places and the people who live there. She brings all these experiences into the classroom and makes us feel that we've visited these places, too. She loved her job, but when she was 43 she had a child and decided that her job was too dangerous for a mother. She also wanted to be near her own mother, who wasn't very well. That's when she made the decision to be a teacher. I'm so happy she did. She's such a warm and positive person that when you're in her lessons you don't even feel you're at school.

WRITING

8 Research a person who is famous for doing charity work. Write a paragraph (about 80–100 words) about him or her. Include the following information:

- who the person is
- what charity work he/she does
- what makes him/her so special

GRAMMAR

Comparative and superlative adjectives (review) `SB p.32`

1 ★☆☆ Complete the table.

Adjective	Comparative	Superlative
big	bigger	0 *the biggest*
1 _____	taller	2 _____
3 _____	4 _____	the prettiest
expensive	5 _____	6 _____
7 _____	more interesting	8 _____
9 _____	10 _____	the most difficult
good	11 _____	12 _____
13 _____	worse	14 _____

2 ★★★ Complete the text with the correct form of the adjectives.

I've just been to see *Gravity* and I can say that it's
0 *the most amazing* _____ (amazing) film I've seen this year.
It's brilliant. The special effects are incredible. They're
1 _____ (realistic) than any other
special effects I've seen. You feel like you're in space
with the actors. I really like space films. I thought *Apollo 13*
was really exciting, but *Gravity* is even
2 _____ (exciting). Sandra Bullock and
George Clooney are two of 3 _____
(professional) actors in Hollywood and they do some of
the 4 _____ (good) work of their careers
in this film. Of course, the fact that George Clooney is
5 _____ (handsome) man in the world
helps! The film is on at the Odeon until Friday. Tickets are
6 _____ (cheap) in the afternoon than in
the evening and the cinema is 7 _____
(empty) then too. But whatever you do, don't miss it!

Pronunciation

Words ending with schwa /ə/

Go to page 118. 🔊

(not) as … as comparatives `SB p.32`

3 ★☆☆ Look at the information about two cinemas. Mark 1–5 T (true) or F (false).

	The Roxy	The Gate
price	£10	£8
number of seats	230	170
friendly staff	★	★★★
age of building	1920	1970
distance from your house	1.2 km	0.7 km
overall experience	★★★	★★★

0 The Roxy is more expensive than the Gate. **T**

1 The Roxy is smaller than the Gate. ☐

2 The Gate isn't as friendly as the Roxy. ☐

3 The Gate is older than the Roxy. ☐

4 The Roxy isn't as close as the Gate. ☐

5 The Roxy isn't as good as the Gate. ☐

4 ★★☆ Complete the sentences about the cinemas using (*not*) *as … as* and the adjectives.

0 The Roxy isn't *as cheap as* (cheap) the Gate.

1 The Roxy _____ (friendly) the Gate.

2 The Gate _____ (big) the Roxy.

3 The Roxy _____ (modern) the Gate.

4 The Gate _____ (far) the Roxy.

5 The Gate _____ (good) the Roxy.

5 ★★★ Complete the second sentence so that it means the same as the first. Use no more than three words.

0 There has never been a film as good as *Titanic*.
Titanic is the _*the best*_ film ever.

1 The film is disappointing compared to the book.
The film isn't _____ the book.

2 *Avatar* is the most successful film of all time.
No film has been _____ *Avatar*.

3 *Despicable Me 2* is funnier than *Despicable Me 1*.
Despicable Me 1 _____ as *Despicable Me 2*.

4 *Spider-Man* and *Superman* are equally bad.
Spider-Man is _____ *Superman*.

Making a comparison stronger or weaker 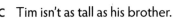 SB p.33

6 ★★☆ Look at the pictures. Mark the sentences ✗ (not true), ✓ (true) or ✓✓ (the best description).

0

Tim
Owen

A	Tim is taller than his brother.	✓
B	Tim is a lot taller than his brother.	✓✓
C	Tim isn't as tall as his brother.	✗

1

143 kg · Floyd
140 kg · Ramsey

A	Floyd is heavier than Ramsey.	
B	Floyd isn't as heavy as Ramsey.	
C	Floyd is a bit heavier than Ramsey.	

2

£100,000
£10

A	B isn't as expensive as A.	
B	B is much more expensive than A.	
C	A is cheaper than B.	

3

Ellie
Ruby

A	Ruby's test was far worse than Ellie's.	
B	Ellie's test was better than Ruby's.	
C	Ellie's test wasn't as good as Ruby's.	

7 ★★★ Complete the sentences so that they are true for you. Use *a lot, much, far, a little* and *a bit*.

0 I *am much shorter than* my best friend.
1 Maths _____ English.
2 Playing sports _____ watching TV.
3 Chocolate _____ apples.
4 Winter _____ summer.
5 Dogs _____ cats.

Adverbs and comparative adverbs SB p.34

8 ★☆☆ Mark the underlined words ADJ (adjective) or ADV (adverb).

0 He plays football <u>worse</u> than I do. *ADV*
1 Her German is <u>better</u> than mine. _____
2 He speaks <u>more clearly</u> than you. _____
3 You walk <u>more quickly</u> than me. _____
4 It's raining a lot <u>harder</u> today. _____

9 ★★☆ Complete the sentences with the correct form of the words in brackets.

'Why can't you be more like your cousin Kevin?' my mum always says.

0 He talks to adults *more politely* (polite) than you.
1 He studies _____ (hard) and always does _____ (good) than you at school.
2 His bedroom is _____ (tidy) than yours.
3 He eats _____ (quick) than you.
4 He writes _____ (careful) than you.
5 He treats me _____ (kind) than you.

GET IT RIGHT! 👁
Comparatives and superlatives

Learners often incorrectly use *better* instead of *best* and *last* instead of *latest*.

✓ Friday is the **best** day of the week.
✗ Friday is the *better* day of the week.
✓ I use the Internet to get the **latest** news.
✗ I use the Internet to get the *last* news.

Circle the correct words.

0 This cinema always shows the *last / latest* films.
1 I don't think pizza is *best / better* than hamburgers.
2 Was it the *last / latest* one left in the shop?
3 It was one of the *best / better* days of my life!
4 He likes to wear the *last / latest* fashion.
5 It's the *best / better* restaurant I know.

VOCABULARY

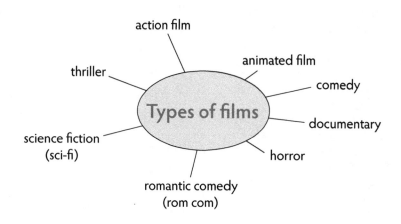

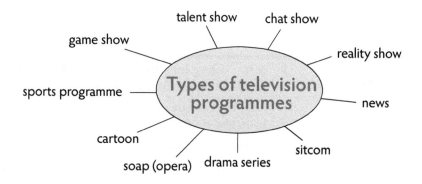

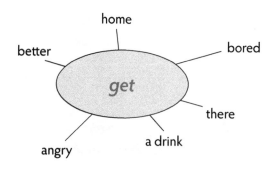

Key words in context

contestant	My mum was a **contestant** on a game show, but she didn't win anything.
crowd	There was a big **crowd** at the football game – more than 50,000 people.
enjoyable	I thought the film was really **enjoyable**. I liked it a lot.
equipment	You can make a film with very little **equipment** – a good video camera is all you need.
extra	They're making a film in my town and they're looking for 500 **extras**.
independent	She's very **independent**. She doesn't want help from anyone.
presenter	My brother is a children's TV **presenter**.
professional	George isn't very **professional**. He's often late for work and never replies to emails.
scary	The film was **scary**. I was really frightened.
scene	My favourite **scene** in the film is when the dragon attacks the castle.
script	The film has a great **script**. It's really well written.

Types of films `SB p.32`

1 ★★☆ **Read the clues and complete the crossword. Who is the mystery film character?**

This type of film ...

0 is often set in the future or in space.

1 is always exciting, with lots of car chases, explosions and special effects.

2 makes you laugh.

3 is exciting and a bit scary at times too.

4 is always scary.

5 tells you about the real world.

6 is popular with children.

7 involves a love story and some laughs.

2 ★★☆ **Read the quotations. Write the type of film you think they come from.**

0 'Quick! We've got 60 seconds to stop the bomb from exploding!' *action film*

1 'Deep in the caves of Colombia lives a bird that few people have ever seen.' _____

2 'The next Mars shuttle leaves at 15.00. Meet me at the space station.' _____

3 'Come on, Barney Bear. We've got a problem to solve.' _____

4 'I love you, Thomas. I've always loved you. You're just too stupid to know that!' _____

5 'Did you see its face? I tell you – that thing isn't human!' _____

6 'It was a rainy Thursday evening in New York – the perfect time for a murder.' _____

7 'Why would I want to be a member of a club that would have me as a member?' _____

Types of television programmes `SB p.35`

3 ★★☆ **Put the letters in order to make types of TV programmes.**

0 thac hows *chat show*

1 swen _____

2 elyairt ohws _____

3 madra eiress _____

4 nocrato _____

5 mage wohs _____

6 cimtos _____

7 opsa proae _____

8 roptss magroprem _____

9 latent whos _____

The crossword:

| 0 | S | C | I | F | I |
| 1 | | | | | |

4 **Write the types of TV programmes.**

WHAT'S ON?

0 'Tonight there's live action from Anfield, where Liverpool play Manchester City.' *sports programme*

1 'Who will win the final of *The It factor*: Janice and her amazing dog Timmy or the boy band Welcome?' _____

2 'On the sofa tonight, answering Paula Nightingale's questions, is actor Lewis James.' _____

3 'Tonight on *Win It Or Lose It*, three more couples compete to win £50,000.' _____

4 'Catch up on today's stories from the UK and around the world. Followed by the weather.' _____

5 'Minnie has a chance to make things right between Ian and James, but will she take it?' _____

WordWise `SB p.37`
Expressions with *get*

5 ★☆☆ **Complete the sentences.**

0 The show doesn't finish until 11 pm, so I don't think we'll get h*ome* before midnight.

1 I don't know how to get t_____ , so I need to look at the map.

2 If you don't want him to get a_____ , don't ask about the football match. They lost again.

3 You look really thirsty. I'll get you a d_____ .

4 After a week in hospital, he got b_____ .

5 It's an exciting film. You won't get b_____ .

6 ★★☆ **What does *get* mean in each sentence?**

0 Call when you get there. *arrive*

1 Don't get too excited. _____

2 I need to get new jeans. _____

3 Where did you get that idea? _____

4 What did you get for your birthday? _____

READING

1 **REMEMBER AND CHECK** Answer the questions. Then check your answers in the article on page 31 of the Student's Book.

0 How much older is *Titanic* than *Spider-Man 3*?   *Titanic is ten years older than Spider-Man 3.*

1 How much cheaper to make was *Titanic* than *Spider-Man 3*? _____

2 How many films did Moviefone consider better than *Monsters* in 2010? _____

3 What was the total cost of the cameras, film, etc. for *Monsters*? _____

4 How many people did it take to make *Monsters*? _____

5 How many main actors are there in the film? _____

6 How long did Edwards spend working on the film after filming? _____

7 How long is *Monsters*? _____

2 Read the web page and comments. Which two films do the comments mainly talk about?

THE MOST EXPENSIVE FILM OF ALL TIME (WELL, UP TO 2012)

1 *John Carter* (2012) – This Walt Disney epic cost around $300 million dollars. Unfortunately, neither critics nor audiences really liked it.

2 *Pirates of the Caribbean – At World's End* (2007) – This third film in the pirate story cost almost $300 million, but made more than three times that around the world.

3 *The Hobbit: An Unexpected Journey* (2012) – Each of the films in this Middle Earth fantasy trilogy cost about $250 million, meaning the total series cost near to $750 million.

4 *Tangled* (2010) – At $260 million, this Disney animation more than doubled its money, as audiences and critics loved it.

5 *Spider-Man 3* (2007) – It cost about $260 million. The critics hated it, but it still made nearly $900 million at the box office.

How can anyone justify spending so much money on a film? There are so many better things we could spend our money on: better roads, housing for everyone, looking after our environment, etc.
Jazzfan

👍 👎   LIKE · COMMENT · SHARE

Jazzfan – you're missing the point. Firstly, it isn't our money. It's the film studio's money, so they can spend it on what they want. Secondly, most of these films (except *John Carter* so far) have gone on to make loads of money for the studio. They're good economic investments.
Cottonbud

Why does it cost so much money to make an animated film? I mean, I really enjoyed *Tangled*, but I can't see how it cost $260 million!
Johnboy

Johnboy – Have you ever seen the credits at the end of an animated film? There are so many people involved. They all need to get paid. Also, they probably paid the storywriters a lot. It costs a lot to get a good story.
Cottonbud

I agree, Cottonbud. The writing in *Tangled* is brilliant. I took my kids to see it thinking it was just a film for children, but I was wrong. As a 35-year-old, I loved it. It made me laugh out loud several times. Much better than any of the other films on this list.
Johnboy

I can't believe they spent so much money on *John Carter*. What a waste of money – all special effects and no story. It was so bad that it made me laugh.
Liam86

Disagree with Liam86. Thought *John Carter* was fabulous – a good old-fashioned adventure film with brilliant special effects. Loved it! It reminded me of the films I watched as a boy. Don't understand why it didn't make any money.
OllieClarke

3 Read the comments again. Mark the sentences T (true) or F (false).

0 Jazzfan doesn't approve of lots of money being spent on a film.   **T**

1 Cottonbud says film studios need to make money. ☐

2 Cottonbud lists three reasons why animated films cost a lot to make. ☐

3 Johnboy was surprised he liked *Tangled*. ☐

4 Johnboy found *Tangled* very funny. ☐

5 Liam86 describes *John Carter* as a comedy. ☐

6 OllieClarke says *John Carter* made him remember his childhood. ☐

4 Choose one of the comments and write a reply (about 20–30 words).

DEVELOPING WRITING

Discursive essay: for and against

1 **Read the essay. Does the writer agree or disagree with the title?** _____

'Watching television is a waste of time.' Discuss.

A Love it or hate it, television is a part of our lives. Parents use it as a babysitter for their children, teenagers watch it so they can discuss it with their friends at school and many old people depend on it for company. We all watch it, but are we really just wasting our time?

B TV is certainly an easy way of passing the time. All we have to do is turn it on and watch. It's easier than reading a book or doing exercise. It can make us lazy and it can become addictive. *Furthermore*, many programmes don't do anything to improve our lives. There are many arguments to support the idea that we waste too much time watching TV.

C *However*, in our busy lives we need time to relax and forget our problems. TV is the perfect way of doing this. *Moreover*, not all programmes on TV are rubbish. There are plenty of programmes that teach us things and make us think. If we choose the right programmes, TV can be a very good use of our time.

D *Personally*, I don't think we can say that watching TV is always a waste of time. Of course, it's very easy to waste a lot of time watching it, time that we could use for doing more useful things. *In my opinion*, if we plan what we watch and keep control over how much we watch, sensible TV viewing can be an important part of our lives.

2 **Look at the words in *italics*. Which …**

1 two expressions are used to say what you think?
   Personally and _____

2 two words are used to add another argument?
   _____ and _____

3 word is used to give an opposing argument? _____

3 **Match the paragraphs with the purposes.**

0	arguments to support the title	B
1	arguments against the title	
2	the writer's own opinion	
3	an introduction to the topic	

4 **Decide whether the arguments refer to statements A or B and whether they are for or against.**

A 'Going to the cinema is always better than watching a DVD at home.'

B 'Film stars get paid too much money.'

		A or B	For	Against
0	They work really hard.	B		✓
1	We need to support our local cinemas.			
2	You can stop and start when you want.			
3	No one should get that amount of money.			
4	They make the film companies a lot of money.			
5	You can watch it as many times as you want.			
6	Films always look better on a big screen.			

5 **Choose a statement from Exercise 4. Write an essay (about 200 words).**

- Your introduction should make an impact. It shouldn't say what your opinion is.
- One paragraph should support the title and one should argue against it.
- Use the conclusion to give your opinion.

LISTENING

1 🔊 13 **Listen to the conversations. Match them with the pictures.**

 **A** 4

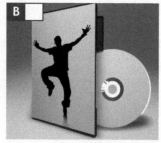 **B**

 **C**

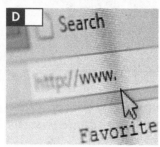 **D**

2 🔊 13 **Listen again and answer the questions.**

0 Why does the man change his mind about getting some help?
   Because he drops the TV and wants to help clear it up.

1 Why can't the man open the web page?

2 What DVD does the shop assistant recommend?

3 Why won't the TV work?

DIALOGUE

1 **Put the words in order to make requests and offers.**

Offers

0 any / help / you / do / need
   Do you need any help ?

1 help / I / you / can
   _____ ?

2 OK / everything / is
   _____ ?

Requests

3 something / you / help / could / with / me
   _____ ?

4 hand / lend / you / me / can / a
   _____ ?

5 few / you / minutes / got / have / a
   _____ ?

2 **Match the offers and requests in Exercise 3 with the replies.**

a No, I'm all right. ☐

b Sure – what is it? ☐

c I do, actually. ☐ *0*

d Not really. I can't get the TV to work. ☐

e Of course I can. ☐

f Sure. Now, let me see. ☐

3 **Write a short conversation about the picture.**

PHRASES FOR FLUENCY

1 **Put the conversation in the correct order.**

☐ **ANNA** I always knew I would be. In fact, I had a dream about it when I was a little girl.

☐ **ANNA** Well, this one did!

1 **ANNA** Guess what? I've got a part in a soap opera!

☐ **ANNA** I am. Have a look. It's a letter from the TV company.

☐ **PAUL** What? You aren't serious!

☐ **PAUL** Oh, come on! Dreams don't mean anything.

☐ **PAUL** Wow! It's true! Looks like you're going to be famous after all.

2 **Complete the conversations with the phrases in the list.**

~~Guess what?~~ | have a look | after all
In fact | Looks like | come on

CONVERSATION 1

A ⁰ *Guess what?* I won the singing competition.

B Oh, ¹_____ ! You aren't a good singer.
   ²_____ , you're terrible!

A You're just jealous.

CONVERSATION 2

A So did you fail the test?

B No, I got 95 per cent!

A What?!

B Here – ³_____ if you don't believe me.

A It's true!

B ⁴_____ I'm not stupid ⁵_____ !

34

Help with listening: getting ready to do a listening activity

1 🔊 14 **Listen to some people talking about their hobbies. Match each of the speakers with two activities. There are two activities you don't need to use.**

1 Joanne   `b` ☐
2 Marek   ☐ ☐
3 Alessandra   ☐ ☐
4 Jorge   ☐ ☐

a going to the theatre
b going swimming
c going to the cinema
d watching films on the computer
e going to the sports centre
f playing a musical instrument
g going shopping
h going cycling
i talking to his/her friends
j writing his/her blog

Exam guide: preparing to listen

When you do a listening activity in class, it's a good idea to do some reading and thinking before you listen, to get yourself ready. Here are some ideas.

- Read the task carefully. Are you sure you know what you have to do?
- Read the list of things carefully. Perhaps say the words to yourself in your head (or aloud if you aren't in class) and picture the things in your mind.
- It can be a good idea to underline the important words (for example, *go to the theatre*). Listen for these words when you listen to the recording.

- Sometimes the words in the task aren't exactly the same as the words you're going to hear. Is there another way you can say, for example, *go cycling* or *go to the cinema*? Try to think of words that are associated with the things written in the task.
- Listening can be challenging. A little work before you listen can help you a lot and make you more confident when you start listening.

Now try Exercise 2. It's a different kind of task – but can you use any of these tips to help you?

2 🔊 15 **You will hear a girl, Maia, talking about television. Decide if each sentence is correct or incorrect. If it's correct, circle the letter A for YES. If it isn't correct, circle the letter B for NO.**

		YES	NO
0	Maia watches a lot of television.	A	Ⓑ
1	Her favourite programme is called *The Street*.	A	B
2	The programme is on two days a week.	A	B
3	All the people in the programme live in the same street.	A	B
4	The person she likes most is called Ted.	A	B
5	The customers in the shop get angry with him because he makes mistakes.	A	B

GRAMMAR

Indefinite pronouns (*everyone*, *no one*, *someone*, etc.) SB p.40

1 ★☆☆ (Circle) the correct words.

> ## The new XR4 has landed!
>
> ○ It's [0] *everything* / *something* you could want in a tablet and more.
>
> ○ It's so simple that [1] *no one* / *anyone* can use it, but if there's [2] *everything* / *anything* you don't understand, our technical team are waiting to help.
>
> ○ Its amazing network coverage means you have Internet access [3] *everywhere* / *somewhere* you go.
>
> ○ If there's [4] *something* / *nothing* you need to remember or somewhere you need to be, the alarm system will make sure you don't forget.
>
> ○ If you order before Christmas, there's [5] *nothing* / *everything* to pay until March.
>
> ○ The new XR4 – [6] *someone* / *no one* should leave home without it.

2 ★★☆ Complete the sentences with the words in the list.

anyone | everyone | nowhere | somewhere
anywhere | anything | no one | something

0   This party's boring. I don't know __anyone__ .

1   I'm sure I've seen that man _____ before, but I can't remember when.

2   Sally's really enjoying her new school. _____ has been so friendly to her.

3   There are no seat numbers in this cinema – you can sit _____ you like.

4   It wasn't me. I didn't do _____ , I promise!

5   Have you spoken to Ian? There's _____ he wants to tell you.

6   There are no trees here, so there's _____ to hide from the sun.

7   It's a secret. Tell _____ !

3 ★★★ Complete the second sentence so that it means the same as the first. Use no more than three words.

0   Liz is really popular. *Everyone* likes Liz.

1   I'm really bored. There's _____ do.

2   Are you hungry? Do you want _____ eat?

3   There's danger everywhere. _____ safe.

4   The cat has disappeared. I can't find _____ .

5   He's following me. He's _____ go.

all / some / none / any of them SB p.41

4 ★☆☆ Match the sentence halves.

0   We've got hundreds of DVDs, but   [c]
1   I've got a lot of pens, but   [   ]
2   There were ten teams in the competition, but [   ]
3   Twenty students took the final test and   [   ]
4   The dogs have already eaten, so   [   ]

a   all of them passed.
b   don't give any of them more food.
c   I've already watched all of them.
d   none of them played very well.
e   I don't think any of them work.

5 ★★☆ Complete the sentences with *all, some, any* or *none*.

0   I have lots of friends, but __none__ of them remembered my birthday.

1   I like most of his films, but _____ of them are awful.

2   I can't say which game I like best. I love _____ of them.

3   I invited all my classmates to the party, but _____ of them came.

4   He's got 2,000 stamps. _____ of them are very rare.

5   Three buses came, but _____ of them were full.

> ## Pronunciation
>
> The short /ʌ/ vowel sound
>
> **Go to page 119.** 🔊

Giving advice: *should(n't), had better, ought to* SB p.43

6 ★☆☆ **Match the sentences with the pictures.**

0 You should buy it. It looks good on you. `C`

1 We ought to leave now. It's going to rain. ☐

2 You'd better see a doctor about that. ☐

3 There's a lot to do. We ought to start now. ☐

4 You shouldn't touch those. They might be hot. ☐

5 We'd better hide – quick! ☐

A

B

C

D

E

F

7 ★★☆ **Write advice using the phrases in the list.**

~~change to a better provider~~ | open it | delete it
attach it as a file | activate flight mode on your tablet
choose a good password for it | upload it onto your blog
go online and find it cheaper

0 My phone never has a signal.
   You'd better change to a better provider.

1 I don't know who this email is from and it's got a strange-looking attachment.
   _____

2 This email's got lots of important information in it.
   _____

3 The new One Direction CD is £15 in the shops!
   _____

4 The plane's about to take off.
   _____

5 This photo's really embarrassing. I don't want anyone to see it.
   _____

6 I need to send this photo to Bob.
   _____

7 This web page contains loads of my personal details.
   _____

GET IT RIGHT!

all vs. *everyone*

Learners sometimes confuse *all* and *everyone*.

Everyone is a pronoun that refers to a group of people.
✓ In the cinema we bought popcorn for **everyone**.
✗ In the cinema we bought popcorn for ~~all~~.

All is used to modify a noun or pronoun.
✓ My family have **all** got mobile phones.
✗ My family have ~~everyone~~ got mobile phones.

Complete the sentences with *everyone* or *all*.

0 I hope *everyone* likes the cake I've made.

1 My friends have _____ got jobs.

2 There should be enough lemonade for us _____ to have some.

3 Has _____ finished their work?

4 Does _____ that you know have a computer?

5 I would like to introduce myself to _____ members personally.

6 After that, _____ of us got a ball and tried to balance it on our heads.

VOCABULARY

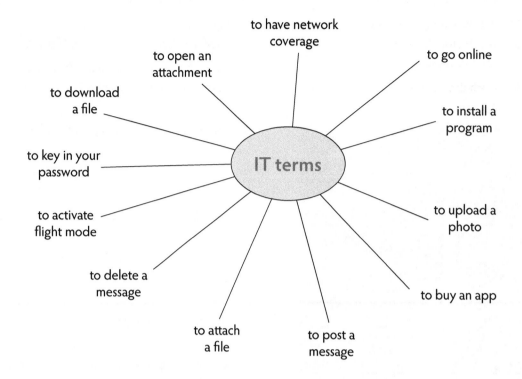

Language for giving advice

bad / good / practical / useful advice
advice on (something)
to ask for / get advice from (someone)
to give / offer (somebody) advice
to take / follow (someone's) advice
to ignore (someone's) advice
advisable
to advise (someone) (to do something)
to advise against (something)

Key words in context

account	I've got two email **accounts**. I use one for work and one for personal emails.
browse	Are you going to buy that book or are you just **browsing** through it?
cave	It was dark inside the **cave** and I couldn't see a thing. Luckily, I had a torch with me.
communication	There's no **communication** between them. They never tell each other anything.
emotion	My dad rarely laughs and I've never seen him cry. He doesn't show any **emotions**.
engrave	He has her name **engraved** on his ring.
get bullied	My sister **got bullied** at school, so she changed to another one.
invention	Is the Internet the greatest **invention** ever?
lick	He **licked** the stamp and put it on the envelope.
printing press	It's the oldest **printing press** in the country. It produced the first books in 1546.
publish	Our school newspaper is **published** every month.
social media	I think I'm the only person in the world who doesn't use any **social media** sites.

IT terms `SB p.40`

1 ★★☆ **Match the sentence halves.**

0 Before take-off, please activate   `d`

1 Don't open that   ☐

2 I haven't got any network   ☐

3 It's already Friday and I haven't posted   ☐

4 If you can't go to the shops, go   ☐

5 To open that file, you need to install   ☐

a   a message on my blog yet.

b   coverage, so I can't make a call.

c   this program first.

d   flight mode on your mobile devices.

e   attachment. It could have a virus.

f   online and buy it.

2 ★★☆ **Complete the sentence with an appropriate verb.**

8 steps to online security

1   Never _____ an attachment if you don't know where it's come from.

2   Think twice before you _____ a message on Facebook.

3   Don't _____ photos of people onto social media sites without asking them.

4   Be careful if you _____ in passwords in a public place.

5   Always _____ emails that you don't want other people to read.

6   Don't _____ apps from online stores you've never heard of.

7   Check what a program is before you _____ it onto your computer.

3 ★★★ **Complete the words.**

1   That's a great photo. You should u<u>pload</u> it to your s_____ m_____ pages.

2   If you like birdwatching, you should b_____ this a_____. It identifies birds from their song.

3   I forgot to a_____ the f_____ before I sent the email.

4   I've deleted the m_____ without reading it.

5   You need enter your email address and then k_____ in your p_____.

6   It takes ages to d_____ big files.

Language for giving advice `SB p.43`

4 ★☆☆ **Write *advise* or *advice*.**

0   Don't take his <u>*advice*</u>. He doesn't know what he's talking about.

1   Our teachers always _____ us not to leave our homework until the last minute.

2   I must _____ you not to call her after 8 pm.

3   My mum always gives me good _____.

5 ★☆☆ (Circle) **the correct option: A, B or C.**

The [0] <u>*most*</u> useful advice I ever got was from my grandfather. He said: 'Never take [1]_____ from anyone.' But I was only 18 and didn't know how good it was, so I [2]_____ his advice and let people give me advice [3]_____ everything. I [4]_____ advice on what to wear and what to eat. My bank manager advised [5]_____ save my money; friends advised me to spend it. My mother advised me to marry young; my father advised me [6]_____ it. I got so much advice [7]_____ so many people that I didn't know which advice to [8]_____ and which advice to ignore. My grandfather was right. Now I've stopped [9]_____ advice and life is much simpler!

0	A more	(B) most	C much
1	A advice	B advise	C advisable
2	A took	B followed	C ignored
3	A on	B in	C over
4	A had got	B got	C had
5	A to me	B me to	C me for
6	A for	B against	C on
7	A from	B for	C with
8	A get	B offer	C follow
9	A taking	B giving	C ignoring

6 ★★☆ **Answer the questions for you.**

1   What are you good at giving advice on?

_____

2   What's the worst advice you've ever got?

_____

3   Whose advice do you always follow and why?

_____

4   Are you good at taking advice? Why (not)?

_____

5   Do you like giving advice? Why (not)?

_____

7 ★★★ **Write about the best advice you ever got (about 50 words). Who gave it to you and why was it good advice?**

READING

1 REMEMBER AND CHECK Complete the sentences. Then check your answers in the article on page 39 of the Student's Book.

0 The man who lost his job because of social networking was ___20___ years old.

1 Around _____ people came to Cathy's party.

2 Every year, about _____ young people create problems for themselves because of social networking.

3 Rule _____ talks about keeping your online information safe.

4 Rule _____ suggests you should think before you post.

5 Rule _____ talks about the importance of good manners online.

2 Read the article. Write the names of the people under the pictures.

1 _____

2 _____

3 _____

3 Read the article again. Answer the questions.

Be careful what you say

These days, with Internet sites like Twitter, it's very easy to let everyone know what you're thinking. But be careful what you say. It might get you into trouble, as it did for these three people.

In January 2010, Paul Chambers was lying in bed with a cold when he saw on TV that Doncaster Airport was closed because of snow. Paul had a flight from the airport the next week. Without really thinking, Paul sent a message on Twitter joking about blowing up the airport if it wasn't open soon. When he went to work on Monday, he found four police officers waiting for him at his office. He thought it was a joke, but when they took him to the police station and locked him up for eight hours, he knew it was serious. He went to court in May and had to pay nearly £1,000 for sending a threatening message.

Journalist Guy Adams was angry with the London Olympics on American TV. Because of the time difference between the US and the UK, the TV station NBC wasn't showing the sport live. Guy decided to tweet the email address of NBC's Head of Olympics, Gary Zenkel. He suggested that his followers tweeted and told Gary what they thought of his decision. When Guy tried to get into his Twitter account two days later, he found it was closed. He got an email a few days later telling him that he was no longer allowed to use the site.

!!! ...

Nicole Crowther was an actress in the popular US musical TV series *Glee*. She was an extra, which meant that although she was often in the show, she never said anything. However, on Twitter she regularly said things. In fact, she started giving away secrets about the programme. When the show's co-creator, Brad Falchuk, saw her tweets, he decided that she couldn't be in the show any longer. Nicole apologised and cancelled her Twitter account, but it was too late. She's now looking for other acting work.

?*@

0 Who tweeted another person's contact details? ___Guy___

1 Who lost a job because of Twitter? _____

2 Who did Twitter ban from using their site? _____

3 Who found themselves in trouble with police because of a tweet? _____

4 Who decided to stop using Twitter after the incident? _____

5 Who worried about the weather? _____

4 Complete the sentence with your ideas.

I think the story about _____ is the most interesting because _____

DEVELOPING WRITING

Computer advice

1 Read the blog entry and complete it with the words in the list.

~~tablet~~ | download | posted | blog | install | machine | deleted | online

Tipps for everyday life

Hi – I'm Johnny Tipp and welcome to my blog.
Everyday life teaches me something. That's why
I started this blog – so I could share it all with you.

Tipp 31 What to do when your computer goes wrong

I'm writing this post on my ^{0} _tablet_ because the desktop computer isn't working at the moment and everyone thinks it's my fault. But as I keep telling them, I was only trying to help.

Let me explain. A few days ago, I was writing my ^{1}_____ when a message appeared on the screen. It said there was a problem with the computer and that I should restart the ^{2}_____ . So I did. After five minutes, the same message appeared again. So I restarted it again. After about five times, I began to think this problem was serious, so I went ^{3}_____ to find a solution. I found a site that promised to fix everything.

TIP 1 You should never trust anyone who promises to fix everything.
All I had to do was ^{4}_____ a file onto my computer and then ^{5}_____ it. So I did.

TIP 2 You should never download files from people who promise to fix everything.
The next thing I saw was a message ^{6}_____ on the screen: 'To fix this problem, please enter your credit card details.' Well, for some reason, I know my dad's credit card details and so I entered them.

TIP 3 Never pay anyone who promises to do everything before they do it.
Then the computer just ^{7}_____ all the files on it and turned itself off and has never come on again since. So when Dad came home, all tired from work, I told him the whole story.

TIP 4 Never tell bad news to a tired person.
When he finally calmed down, he rang his bank. They found that £1,000 was missing from his account.

And that's it. It was an expensive lesson, but I've learned a lot.
PS I'm not the most popular person in my house at the moment.

2 Read the blog entry again. Put the events in order.

- [ ] Johnny tells his dad about the problem.
- [ ] Johnny writes his blog.
- [ ] Johnny installs a program.
- [1] Johnny's computer tells him it has a problem.
- [ ] Johnny's computer completely breaks down.
- [ ] Johnny goes online to try and find a solution.
- [ ] Johnny uses his dad's credit card.
- [ ] Johnny downloads a program.

3 Write a blog entry giving advice to your readers (about 200–300 words). Tick (✓) the checklist.

- [ ] 200–300 words
- [ ] chatty, informal language
- [ ] contains advice
- [ ] interesting content
- [ ] nothing too personal

Writing tip: writing a blog

- A blog is something that someone writes because they want to share some information with the rest of the world. Some blogs are about specific topics such as cycling or online gaming. Others are just about the everyday life of the author.
- Decide what your blog will be about. Do you have a special interest in something that you would like to share or do you just want to talk about your life?
- Your blog should be interesting. If it isn't, it won't attract many readers.
- If your blog is about your life, be careful not to give away personal information such as your address or phone number.
- Keep your blog chatty and informal. Write in a style that is appropriate to your readers.
- If you want to keep your readers, don't forget to update your blog regularly.

LISTENING

1 🔊 17 **Listen to the conversations. Match them with the computer screens.**

A ☐   B ☐   Error 323   C ☐

2 🔊 17 **Listen again and complete the notes.**

CONVERSATION 1
Problem: *The program keeps freezing.*
Solution: _____

CONVERSATION 2
Problem: _____
Solution: _____

CONVERSATION 3
Problem: _____
Solution: _____

3 🔊 17 **Listen again and answer the questions.**

CONVERSATION 1

1   What kind of computer does the man have?

_____

CONVERSATION 2

2   What kind of computer does the man have?

_____

3   When did the man buy it?

_____

CONVERSATION 3

4   What is the man's password?

_____

5   What does the man see on his screen?

_____

DIALOGUE

1   Put the words in order to make sentences.

0   we'll / better / do / shop / and / bring / the /
    machine / can / You'd / into / the / see / we / what
    You'd better bring the machine into
    the shop and we'll see what we can do.

1   read / use / You / to / you / computer / the / ought /
    before / instructions / really / the

_____

2   anyone / tell / should / never / password / You / your

_____

3   put / immediately / your / down / You / the /
    should / phone / call / bank / and

_____

TRAIN TO THiNK

Logical sequencing

1   Put the actions into a logical order.

1

☐ Ask for some advice
☐ Get some bad advice
☐ Take the advice
☒ *1* Have a problem
☐ Get some good advice
☐ Ignore the advice
☐ Ask someone else

2

☐ Send your message
☐ Write a reply
☐ Add an attachment
☐ Delete the first message
☐ Log into your email
☐ Key in your password
☒ *1* Go online
☐ Read a message

2   Connect the first and last events in the lists with your own ideas.

1

1   Find an old friend on a social networking site.
2   *Send the friend a message asking*
    about their life.
3   _____
4   _____
5   Delete the friend!

2

1   See a great new band on TV.
2   _____
3   _____
4   _____
5   Go and see their show.

Reading part 2

Exam guide: matching people with activities and things

- In this question you have to read short descriptions of five people and match them with the best options. The options relate to a particular subject, for example, the best holiday location, the film they'll like the most or the museum they'll find the most interesting.
- Read through the short descriptions of each person. Underline the important information in each one.
- Before you read through the options, think about what sort of thing you would recommend for each person.
- Read through the options and underline the most important information in each one. See if any match your own ideas.
- Beware of 'word spotting'. Just because the same word might appear in the description and one of the options, it doesn't always mean that this is a match. For example, just because Tom is going to India, it doesn't mean that theheartofindia.com is necessarily the best place for him.
- Always double-check and look carefully at all the information. Look out for traps. For example, Andy is looking for a recipe for hot and spicy food and goodenoughtoeat.com offers this, so you might think this is the perfect match. But look again. Andy wants to make a beef dish and this website is for vegetarians!
- Remember: there are always three extra options. These extra options will usually contain traps.

1 Match the people 1–5 with five of the websites A–H.

1 Liam is doing a school Geography project. He has to find out all he can about Russia, China, Brazil and India, and use the information to compare these countries. ☐

2 Tom is going on a two-month trip around India. He knows exactly what he wants to see and do, but he needs to organise how he's going to get around and where he's going to stay. ☐

3 Andy is cooking dinner for some friends tonight. He wants to make a spicy beef dish and needs a good recipe. ☐

4 Olivia has got to look after her two young children during the school holidays. She wants to find things to do in the local area that will get them out of the house. ☐

5 Miriam is taking her niece for a day out to the science museum in Manchester. She wants to drive there, but has no idea how to get there. ☐

HOT SITES – A pick of the best new websites this week

A fromAtoBandback.com
Everything from road directions to bus and train timetables. Just type in where you are and where you want to go and we'll tell you the best way of getting there. We also work out how long it'll take you to get there and how much it'll cost. You'll never need to feel lost again.

B goodenoughtoeat.com
Transform your carrots, cabbages, onions and mushrooms into wonderful meals that all the family will love. From soups to keep you warm in the winter to hot, spicy curries to impress your friends at any time of the year. We have a vegetarian recipe for every occasion. Say goodbye to meat!

C theheartofindia.com
India is one of the world's oldest and most magical civilisations. Our site is dedicated to 1,000 years of tradition. Everything you'll ever need to know about India is here: our history, our customs, our stories, our cities, our wildlife and our people. You'll also find the best recipes for curries anywhere on the web!

D wotson.com
Looking for a good film to see or show to go to? Want to know what exhibitions are on at the museums and art galleries in your area? Are there any special events taking place near you this weekend? Check out what's happening around you this month here.

E rentacar.com
If you're just looking for a small car for the day or a more luxurious model for the month, you won't find a better deal than here. Our cars all come freshly cleaned, full of petrol and with a satnav, so you'll always know where you are. For the best prices in town – we can't be beaten.

f thejourneyplanner.com
No matter where in the world you're going, we have all the information you'll need to plan the perfect holiday. Our site also searches the Internet to give you the best prices on accommodation, transport and eating out. Our simple booking form makes it easy for you to make all your reservations and take all the worry out of arriving.

g rainyday.com
Kids home for the summer? Rain pouring down outside? Don't worry. We have hundreds of ideas to keep your children active over the holidays. Perfect for those days when getting out of the house seems impossible. Turn off the TV and get busy.

h welcometotheworld.com
The Internet database for all 196 countries in the world. Facts and figures on everything from population size to life expectancy, from import and export to GDP. Find out how your country compares to the rest of the world.

CONSOLIDATION

LISTENING

1 🔊 18 **Listen to the conversation. Tick (✓) A, B or C.**

1 What kind of show is *Priceless*?
   A a chat show ☐
   B a sports show ☐
   C a game show ☐

2 What kind of film is *Let Him Go*?
   A a sci-fi film ☐
   B a horror film ☐
   C a comedy film ☐

3 What time does the *Let Him Go* start?
   A 8 pm ☐
   B 9 pm ☐
   C 11 pm ☐

2 🔊 18 **Listen again. Answer the questions.**

0 Why does Jim want to stay in?
   Because he's a bit tired.

1 What day of the week is it?
   _____

2 What kind of film is *By Tomorrow*?
   _____

3 What happens in *Let Him Go*?
   _____

4 What does Sally want Jim to make?
   _____

VOCABULARY

3 **Look at the word snake. Find 12 types of films and TV programmes and write them in the correct column. Some can go in both.**

scifidocomedyeschatshowdenewstethrilleroooromcommidocumentaryosdramatrseriessitcomehorrorfilmsesoapoperanacartoon

TV shows	Types of films
	sci-fi

4 **Complete the text with the words in the list. There are three words you don't need.**

~~buy~~ | download | attach | useful | on | post against | open | ignored | for | followed | key

One of the problems with modern technology is the number of passwords you need to remember. Every time I want to ⁰ *buy* an app, check my email or ¹ _____ a message on Facebook, I have to ² _____ in a password. My computer even sometimes asks for one if I want to ³ _____ a file or ⁴ _____ an attachment. What makes it worse is that all these passwords have to be different. So I asked a friend of mine ⁵ _____ some advice. He advised me ⁶ _____ keeping them on my computer. He told me to write them all down in a file and send it to myself and keep it in my email inbox. It sounded like ⁷ _____ advice so I ⁸ _____ it and did exactly what he said. So my passwords are all safely stored in my email inbox. The only problem is that I can't remember the password to access it!

GRAMMAR

5 **Rewrite the sentences using the words in brackets.**

0 I don't know anyone kinder than her. (kindest)
   She's the kindest person I know.

1 The film was hated by everyone. (no one)
   _____

2 You should study more if you've got a test tomorrow. (better)
   _____

3 The weather was a lot nicer yesterday. (worse)
   _____

4 Polly is nearly as tall as Angus. (a bit)
   _____

5 The best thing for you to do is to tell the truth. (ought)
   _____

6 Is this house empty? (anyone)
   _____

7 I'm a bad singer, but I'm better than Josh. (badly)
   _____

8 It's really important for me to finish this today. (must)
   _____

9 It's a good idea for us to leave early. (need)
   _____

DIALOGUE

6 Complete the conversation. Use the phrases in the list.

~~have you got a few minutes?~~ | looks like
Is everything OK? | Can you lend me a hand?
ought to | after all | I can do it for you
have a look | In fact

EMMA	Simon, ⁰ *have you got a few minutes?*
SIMON	Sure. Yes, I have. ¹_____
EMMA	Not really. I'm trying to download this file, but it isn't working. ²_____
SIMON	Of course. Let me take a look.

[after a few minutes]

SIMON	That's very strange. It ³_____ you've got a virus on your computer.
EMMA	A virus!
SIMON	Yes, ⁴_____. Each time I try and open this window, it just shuts down.
EMMA	Oh no. Is it serious?
SIMON	Not really. ⁵_____, I had the same one on my computer. I know exactly what to do.
EMMA	Great. So can you fix it?
SIMON	Yes, I can. I'm just running a program now. But you really ⁶_____ update your virus protection. ⁷_____ if you want.
EMMA	Thanks. That would be great.
SIMON	Oh. Oh dear.
EMMA	What?
SIMON	Well, it didn't do that before. It seems your computer's gone completely dead. Very strange. Maybe I didn't know that virus ⁸_____ .

READING

7 Read the article and match the missing sentences with the spaces A–F. There is one sentence that you don't need.

0	they watched the night before	B
1	in the house	☐
2	apart from things like live football matches,	☐
3	like they did when my parents were children	☐
4	whenever and wherever they like	☐
5	better sound and	☐
6	you didn't have a chance of seeing it again	☐

The end of television?

Does anybody sit down and watch TV these days? When my parents were growing up, they only had a few channels to choose from. If you missed your favourite programme, it was just bad luck – [A] (unless you had a video recorder and remembered to programme it). The TV was the centre point of the house. Families planned what show they wanted to see and cooked their dinners so that they could finish eating in time to watch it. At school, children talked about the shows [B] and because there weren't many programmes for kids, they all watched the same thing.

When I grew up, the TV was bigger and a lot thinner than the TVs of my parents' time. It had [C] a remote control to change between the many channels. But the TV was still an important piece of furniture [D] and we all sat around it on a Saturday night to watch something as a family.

These days, TV just doesn't seem to be so important, and [E] people can choose what they want to watch and when they want to watch it. They don't even need to watch it on a TV. They can download programmes and watch them on their tablets and phones [F]. Watching TV has become a much more individual activity and in many houses the TV set sits forgotten in the corner of the living room, waiting for the day when the family sits down together again and turns it on.

WRITING

8 Write a short text (about 120–150 words) about your favourite TV programme. Include the following information:

- what it is
- when it's on
- what it's about
- why you like it

5 | MY LIFE IN MUSIC

GRAMMAR
Present perfect continuous SB p.50

1 ★☆☆ **Match the sentences with the pictures.**

0 He's been talking to them for hours. **B**

1 He's been waiting for a long time. ☐

2 It's been snowing for days. ☐

3 She's been running for 62 hours. She's trying
   to break the world record. ☐

4 They've been watching TV all evening. ☐

5 She's been playing her favourite instrument
   all morning. ☐

2 ★★☆ **Complete the sentences. Use the present
perfect continuous (positive or negative) form of
the verbs.**

0 She'*s been reading* (read) that book for more
   than a week now.

1 Dave's in bed. He _____ (feel) well for
   about three hours.

2 Dinner's going to be good. Dad _____
   (cook) all afternoon.

3 What awful weather. It _____ (rain) all day.

4 She looks really tired. She _____ (sleep)
   very well.

5 I _____ (study), so I don't think I'm going to
   pass this test.

3 ★★☆ **Complete the text. Use the present
perfect continuous form of the verbs in the list.**

~~try~~ | think | write | talk | dream

I ⁰ *'ve been trying* to contact you. Is your phone
broken? I want to ask you a question: will you join
'The Cool Four'? Jason, Nora, Zoë and I have started
a band! As you know, I ¹_____ songs for years,
and I ²_____ of having my own band. I'm
sure people ³_____ that I'd never do it. Well,
they're wrong! Jason, Nora and Zoë are here now, and
we ⁴_____ about the name of the band if you
join us! How does 'The Cool Five' sound?

4 ★★☆ **Write present perfect continuous
questions.**

0 ☐ *e* why / she / cry
   Why has she been crying _____ ?

1 ☐ how long / she / speak / to the teacher
   _____ ?

2 ☐ how long / you / try to phone me
   _____ ?

3 ☐ what / you / do
   _____ ?

4 ☐ how long / Bob / practise / the piano
   _____ ?

5 ★★★ **Complete the sentences. Use the present
perfect continuous form of the verbs.**

a He'*s been playing* (play) since 10.30.

b I _____ (try) to reach you for two days.

c They _____ (discuss) the exam for an hour.

d I _____ (tidy) my room.

e She _____ (feel) sad about her cat.

6 ★★★ **Match the questions in Exercise 4 with the
answers in Exercise 5. Write a–d in the boxes.**

Pronunciation

Strong and weak forms /biːn/
and /bɪn/

Go to page 119. 🔊

Present perfect simple vs. present perfect continuous SB p.53

7 ★☆☆ **Match 1–5 with a–f.**

0 He's been wearing these jeans for years. ☐ *f*
1 He's bought a new pair of jeans. ☐
2 She's been recording since 7 am. ☐
3 She's recorded all the songs for her new CD. ☐
4 They've been playing all evening. ☐
5 They've played concerts in many countries. ☐

a She's tired and hungry.
b They've got fans all over the world.
c But they're too big for him.
d But they haven't played their best song yet.
e She can go home now.
f He needs to buy a new pair.

8 ★★☆ **Complete the sentences. Use the present perfect simple or present perfect continuous.**

0 We*'ve been practising* all afternoon.
  We *'ve practised* 20 songs. (practise)
1 We _____ at photos for hours.
  We _____ at all my albums! (look)
2 She _____ 50 messages today! She _____ emails since 8 o'clock. (write)
3 We _____ to songs all evening.
  We _____ to five albums. (listen)
4 They _____ the guitar since 1985.
  They _____ a lot of concerts. (play)
5 She _____ 300 pictures. She _____ for many years. (paint)

9 ★★★ **Write questions with *How long* and the present perfect simple or continuous.**

0 you / play / the piano
  How long have you been playing the piano ?
1 he / know / Ben
  _____ ?
2 they / play / in a band
  _____ ?
3 you / have / your guitar
  _____ ?
4 she / listen / to music
  _____ ?
5 they / be / teachers
  _____ ?
6 we / live / in this house
  _____ ?

10 ★★★ **Complete the questions. Use the correct form of the verbs in the list.**

~~know~~ | hear | be | play | study

0 How long *have you known* your best friend?
1 What's your favourite sport and how long _____ it?
2 What class are you in now and how long _____ in it?
3 How long _____ English?
4 What is the most interesting information you _____ today?

11 ★★★ **Write your answers to the questions.**

0 _____
1 _____
2 _____
3 _____
4 _____

GET IT RIGHT! 👁
Present perfect continuous vs. past continuous

Learners sometimes use the past continuous when the present perfect continuous is required.

✓ *I've been looking* for a new phone since last week.
✗ *I was looking* for a new phone since last week.

Complete the sentences with the correct form of the verb in brackets.

0 Over the last few weeks I *'ve been training* (train) for the race.
1 I _____ (eat) breakfast when I heard the news.
2 I _____ (wait) to see the latest *Star Wars* film for months.
3 She _____ (work) there last year, but she left in December.
4 I _____ (play) the violin for two years.
5 We _____ (get) this discount for the last three years.
6 I had to leave the meeting because my mobile phone _____ (ring).

VOCABULARY

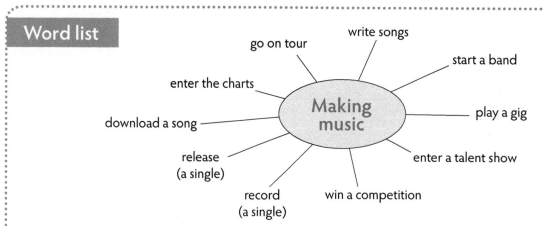

go on tour
write songs
enter the charts
start a band
download a song
Making music
play a gig
release (a single)
enter a talent show
record (a single)
win a competition

Musical instruments

drums

bass guitar

saxophone

piano

violin

trumpet

keyboards

guitar

out

My dad **started out** making tea for the bosses. Now he's the boss of the company.

I only **found out** about his accident when I read about it in the paper.

The printer's **run out** of ink. We need to buy some more.

The new Minecraft game **comes out** next Friday. I can't wait.

Do you want to **go out** tonight? The cinema or a restaurant, maybe?

If you tell me what the problem is, we can **sort it out** together.

Key words in context

busking	In summer you'll hear a lot of **busking** in the streets of London.
concentrate	Music helps me to **concentrate** better on my work.
dance music	I like the rhythm of this song. I think it's good **dance music**.
entertaining	His performances are always very **entertaining**.
jazz	It was black people in the US who invented **jazz**.
lyrics	I don't understand the **lyrics** of this song. What do you think they mean?
melody	I like the **melody** of this song. It's really easy to sing along to.
musician	He's an excellent **musician**. He plays six instruments.
opera	Janet loves classical music, but she doesn't often listen to **opera**.
performance	It was a great **performance** by the band.
pop	What's your favourite **pop** song?
rap	In **rap**, they don't sing the words – they speak them.
rock	I prefer **rock** to pop.

Making music SB p.50

1 ★☆☆ **Complete the text with the words in the list.**

started a band | wrote / songs | recorded / single
download | played gigs | entered the charts
released | went on / tour

When Mick Jagger [0] *started a band* called The Rolling Stones in 1962 with a few friends, he had no idea how successful they would become. The Stones [1]_____ their first _____, *Come On*, a song by the singer Chuck Berry, and [2]_____ it on 7 June, 1963. They never performed it when they [3]_____ because it wasn't 'their' song. But their fans found out about the record, and so many people bought it that it [4]_____ in the UK and went to number 21. Of course, in those days, fans had to go to record shops; they couldn't just [5]_____ music from the Internet! Mick Jagger and Keith Richards [6]_____ a lot of _____ that became very famous. In 1964, The Rolling Stones [7]_____ their first _____ of the US. When they came back, they had their first number one hit in the UK, *It's All Over Now.*

Musical instruments SB p.53

2 ★☆☆ **Put the letters in order to make musical instruments.**

1 The *drums* (sdmur) and the _____ (sabs aitugr) are responsible for the rhythm in a band.

2 The _____ (rmutpte) and the _____ (nxohpasoe) are wind instruments.

3 _____ (ysedbaokrs) are electronic instruments similar to a _____ (iaopn).

4 The _____ (linvoi) and the _____ (griuat) are both examples of string instruments.

3 ★★☆ **Tick (✓) the sentences that are true for you. Correct the ones that aren't.**

1 I never listen to jazz. ☐

_____

2 I prefer pop to rock. ☐

_____

3 I like songs with good melodies. ☐

_____

4 I don't really like rap. ☐

_____

5 I never listen to the lyrics of a song. ☐

_____

WordWise SB p.55

Phrasal verbs with *out*

4 ★☆☆ **Circle the correct option: A, B or C.**

0 We need help. Who could _____ this out for us?
  A come B start Ⓒ sort D go

1 I'm afraid I'm _____ out of ideas. I'm not sure what to do.
  A coming B running C sorting D finding

2 I love _____ out with my friends.
  A finding B starting C sorting D going

3 My cousin _____ out writing for the local newspaper. Now he's a journalist on TV.
  A started B found C sorted D went

4 Nobody saw what happened, so it's difficult for the police to _____ out the truth.
  A come B run C go D find

5 They haven't had a new song for two years, but their new CD should _____ out soon.
  A sort B find C go D come

5 ★★☆ **Match the questions and answers.**

0 Why won't you join us at the cinema tonight? [c]

1 What if your dad finds out about it? ☐

2 When did this book come out? ☐

3 What was your brother's first job? ☐

4 Can I talk to Jane? ☐

5 We have a real problem with this. ☐

a I can't remember. I bought it a long time ago.

b Oh, don't worry. I'm sure we'll sort it out.

c I've run out of money. I just can't afford to go.

d Sorry. She's gone out with her sisters.

e Well, he won't be happy, that's for sure.

f He started out as a drummer.

6 ★★★ **Answer the questions about you.**

1 How often do you go out in a week?

_____

2 Do you know somebody who's good at sorting out problems? How does he/she do it?

_____

3 Do you often buy music that's just come out?

_____

4 How do you find out what songs are cool?

_____

READING

1 **REMEMBER AND CHECK** Answer the questions. Then check your answers in the online forum on page 49 of the Student's Book.

0   What does winning *The X Factor* probably guarantee?   *At least one hit album.*

1   What doesn't it guarantee?

2   What have Justin Bieber and Lily Allen's careers got in common?

3   How did Scooter Brown discover Justin Bieber?

4   What is busking?

5   Where did Eric Clapton busk before he became famous?

2 Read the article quickly. What is the name of the singer? What are the names of his first two albums? Were they successful?

A young man dreams of a career in music. He gets a chance to record two albums, but they don't sell. For many years, he lives on very little money. He has no idea that in the meantime his songs have become extremely popular in other countries, and that his fans believe he's dead.

It sounds like the stuff that fairy tales are made of, but it isn't. It's an incredible but true story and this is only the half of it.

Sixto Rodriguez was the son of Mexican immigrants to the US. He released his first album, *Cold Fact*, in 1970, and his second, *Coming from Reality*, a year later. But nobody bought his music, so he had to do all kinds of jobs to survive. Life was hard for him and his family.

In the meantime, his music was becoming a huge success in three countries on the other side of the

world: Australia, New Zealand and, in particular, South Africa. There, Rodriguez was a huge star, more popular than the Rolling Stones. But there were rumours that he was dead, and he himself had no idea about the success of his music.

Then, finally, in December 1994, 28 years after he released *Cold Fact*, a young South African fan named Stephen 'Sugar' Segerman and Craig Bartholomew, a journalist, wanted to find out more about Rodriguez. They started a website called The Great Rodriguez Hunt, and had his face put on milk cartons in the US, with the question 'Have you seen this man?'. Rodriguez's daughter saw one and the rest is rock history.

In March 1998, he was invited on a big tour across South Africa. Rodriguez played six concerts all over the country, in stadiums filled with thousands of

young people who knew every word to every one of his songs.

In 2012, Swedish film maker Malik Bendjelloul released the documentary film *Searching for Sugar Man*. When the film got a nomination for an Oscar, the director asked Rodriguez to come to the ceremony, but he refused because he feared all the attention would be on him and not the film-makers. The film has helped to make his music successful around the world, but Rodriguez has remained very modest. He's been living in the same simple house in Detroit for 40 years, and he doesn't have a car, a mobile phone or a TV.

3 Read the article again. Mark the sentences A (right), B (wrong) or C (doesn't say).

0   Sixto Rodriguez's parents were Mexican and he was born in Detroit, US.   `C`

1   Lots of people knew his music in South Africa. ☐

2   His daughter put a picture of him on milk cartons. ☐

3   Twenty-eight years after *Cold Fact*, he played in front of thousands of fans in South Africa. ☐

4   Many people knew the lyrics of his songs. ☐

5   The film about Rodriguez got a nomination for an Oscar, but it didn't win. ☐

4 When she saw the advert, Rodriguez's daughter called Stephen 'Sugar' Segerman. Use your imagination to write the first six lines of that phone call.

DAUGHTER   Hello, is that Stephen Segerman?

SEGERMAN

DAUGHTER

SEGERMAN

DAUGHTER

SEGERMAN

DEVELOPING WRITING

A magazine article

1 **Read the article quickly. Answer the questions.**

0 What's the singer's real name?

Ella Yelich-Amidst

1 Where did she grow up?

_____

2 What do experts think of her?

_____

3 What does the writer think of her?

_____

Young and world famous

A In 2013 a song called 'Royals' made a young singer called Lorde famous all over the world. Lorde (real name Ella Marija Lani Yelich-O'Connor) grew up in New Zealand. She is the daughter of a Croatian father and an Irish mother, and has got a younger brother and two sisters. Her unique talent was discovered when she was 12, and she started writing songs when she was 13.

B Ever since Lorde appeared on TV screens for the first time, critics have been praising her fantastic voice, her feel for the rhythm and the music, and also her lyrics. Her mother, herself a poet, encouraged her to read books from an early age, and that is probably what has made the young singer such a good lyrics writer. She says her love for words has been at least as important as her love for music, and both have helped her enormously to become the star she now is.

C Lorde is very young. She became a star when she was 17, and has had a number of successful songs since then. Among them are 'Royals' and 'Tennis Court', which was released in the UK just after the Wimbledon women's final in 2013.

D I have been fascinated by Lorde's music and her personality since I first saw and heard her in a video clip on the Internet. Her songs make me happy. When I hear 'Royals' on the radio, I turn up the music and sing along. I am sure she will have many more hits.

2 **Complete the sentences. Use the correct form of the verbs.**

0 She _**started**_ (start) writing songs when she was 13.

1 Ever since Lorde _____ (appear) on TV screens for the first time, experts _____ (praise) her talent.

2 I _____ (be) fascinated by Lorde's music and personality since I first _____ (see) her in a video clip.

3 **Look at the sentences in Exercise 2. Find examples of verb forms which refer to ...**

0 something that happened at a specific time in the past.

She started writing songs when she was 13.

1 something that started in the past, and is still continuing.

_____

2 how long something has been happening.

_____

4 **Which paragraph of the text talks about ...**

0 the artist's history? | A |
1 examples of her songs? | ☐ |
2 what experts say about her? | ☐ |
3 the writer's personal opinion? | ☐ |

5 **Plan an article about a writer or a musician alive today. Use the questions and tips to help you.**

- Who do you want to write about?
- Find out about the artist's life.
- Find out about the artist's personal situation.
- What do experts think about the artist's success?
- What's your personal opinion?

6 **Write a magazine article about a musician or a singer (about 190 words). Use the article and Exercise 5 to help you.**

LISTENING

1 🔊20 **Listen to the conversations and answer the questions.**

CONVERSATION 1

0 What do William's friends like that he doesn't?
   Listening to music while doing other things.

1 Why can't he listen to music while he's doing something else?

_____

2 When does he like to listen to music?

_____

CONVERSATION 2

3 How does Chloë feel about music?

_____

4 Do her teachers allow her to listen to music during the lessons?

_____

5 How does music make her feel?

_____

CONVERSATION 3

6 Where does Ryan find new music?

_____

7 What are his favourite types of music?

_____

8 Does he listen to music when he works?

_____

DIALOGUE

1 🔊20 **Match the questions and answers. Then listen again and check.**

0 Why's that? | d |
1 So do you never listen to music? | |
2 Does it relax you? | |
3 Could you be without music? | |
4 Do you dance a lot? | |
5 When do you listen to that? | |

a Yeah, it helps me see pictures.

b Not as often as I'd like to.

c Well, when I need to think.

d Because I can't concentrate on both things.

e No, I don't think I could.

f No – I do. I quite like music.

PHRASES FOR FLUENCY

1 **Put the conversation in the correct order.**

	EMMA	It's The Fall – they're playing in the town hall on Saturday.
	EMMA	Why don't we invite Gavin to come along?
1	EMMA	Dan, Dan!
	EMMA	Why not? He loves them.
	EMMA	Well, if you say so. It's just me and you, then.
	EMMA	Yes, really. I've already got my tickets. I can't wait! It's going to be the show of the year.
	DAN	Tell me about it. They're my favourite band. I'm definitely going too.
	DAN	Gavin? No way.
	DAN	What's up, Emma?
	DAN	What?! Really?
	DAN	Listen, there's no point in trying to change my mind. Gavin and I ... well, we just don't like each other. I'd rather not invite him.

2 **Complete the conversations with the expressions in the list.**

~~if you say so~~ | there's no point in | I can't wait
no way | tell me about it | what's up

0
A Stephen King is the best writer in the world.
B *If you say so*. I prefer Jane Austen.

1
A I've told her again and again that she's wrong.
B _____ talking to her. She just won't listen.

2
A Wow, that lesson was boring.
B _____. I almost fell asleep twice!

3
A Let's climb that tree.
B _____. That's far too dangerous.

4
A Hey, Tom. I need to talk to you.
B OK, Julian. _____?

5
A I'm so happy it'll be summer soon.
B Me too. _____ to go swimming.

Listening for specific information

1 🔊21 **Eduardo is thinking about having English lessons. Listen and complete the information.**

THE LIMES SCHOOL OF ENGLISH

COURSE A:
Lessons every 0 _Monday_ and 1 _____
Number of lessons per week: 2 _____
Length of lessons: 3 _____ minutes
Cost: 4£ _____ per week

COURSE B:
Lessons every 5 _____ and _____
Number of lessons per week: 6 _____
Length of lessons: 7 _____ minutes
Cost: 8£ _____ per week

Exam guide: completing notes

- Sometimes, in class or in an examination, you have to listen to something and get specific information. It could be, for example, people's names, or numbers, or a time, or dates, or a price, and so on.
- It's important to look carefully at the task before the listening starts.
- Read the questions and instructions carefully. What kind of information does the question ask you to find? A date? A time? A name? A place?
- You don't need to understand everything in the recording. Look at the questions and listen carefully for the answers. It might be frustrating if you don't understand everything, but remember – you only need to identify certain things in order to do the task successfully.

- Look at the listening exercises on this page. What kind of information did you need to do Task 1? And what kind of information do you need for Task 2? It isn't usually possible to be 100 per cent sure about your predictions, though. For example, think about Task 2, answer 7. What kinds of things might a hotel not accept? Children? Credit cards? Pets?
- Remember that you'll probably hear some information that you don't need. For example, in Task 1, you hear the price of each lesson, but you don't have to write it down for the task. Also, you don't need to write down how many lessons there are each day – only how many lessons each week.
- It's possible that the information you want doesn't come in the same order as in the task. There's an example of this in Task 2.

2 🔊22 **Jean phones a bed and breakfast. Listen and complete the information.**

Sea View Bed and Breakfast

- Single room: 0£ _110_ per night
- Double room: 1£ _____ per night
- All rooms have 2 _____ and 3 _____ .

- Check-in time: 4 _____
- Check-out time: 5 _____
- Car park: 6£ _____ per night
- Sorry, we don't accept 7 _____ .

GRAMMAR

will (not), may (not), might (not) for prediction SB p.58

1 ★☆☆ **Match the sentences with the pictures.**

A   B   C   D   E   F

0	Mum won't be happy when she sees her car.	F
1	Mum will be happy when she sees her car.	
2	Don't eat it all. You'll be ill.	
3	Don't eat it. It might be poisonous.	
4	She may not finish her book tonight.	
5	She won't finish her book tonight.	

2 ★☆☆ **Complete the sentences. Use *will* or *won't* and the verbs in the list.**

~~be~~ | cost | like | believe | get | remember

0   He's grown a lot. He _will be_ taller than me soon.

1   Wow! They _____ me when I tell them!

2   I don't know how much this DVD _____ .

3   The cake is for Jill. I'm sure she _____ it.

4   Don't worry. I _____ there as soon as I can.

5   Listen carefully. Otherwise you _____ what I tell you.

3 ★★☆ Circle **the correct words.**

0   I'm nervous. Mum *might* / *won't* get angry.

1   Wait there. I *'ll* / *might* be two minutes.

2   I don't know the answer. Who *won't* / *might* know?

3   Both teams are good. I've got no idea who *will* / *won't* win.

4   It's getting late. We *may* / *may not* miss the train.

5   I'll tell you, but you *might* / *won't* believe me.

6   They probably *won't* / *might not* come at all.

4 ★★★ **Write predictions using suitable modal verbs.**

0   there / be / no cars / 20 years from now (certainty)
   There will be no cars 20 years from now.

1   we / visit / the US / next summer (possibility)
   _____

2   I / watch / film / in English / next week (possibility)
   _____

3   they / not see / a match / on Sunday (certainty)
   _____

4   next month / there / be / a lot of rain (possibility)
   _____

5   Jim / go / to university / one day (certainty)
   _____

6   Sally / watch TV / tonight (possibility)
   _____

5 ★★★ **Tick (✓) the predictions in Exercise 4 that are true for you. Change the others so that they are true for you.**

0 ☐ _____
1 ☐ _____
2 ☐ _____
3 ☐ _____
4 ☐ _____
5 ☐ _____
6 ☐ _____

6 ★★★ **Write six sentences about the future of your country. Use *will, won't, might (not)* and *may (not)*.**

First conditional; *unless* in first conditional sentences `SB p.61`

7 ★☆☆ (Circle) the correct words.

0 If I *see* / *'ll see* her again, I'll tell her to phone you.

1 We won't go on holiday if Dad *is* / *will be* still ill.

2 If you *won't* / *don't* talk about it, nobody will know.

3 *Will* / *Do* they want to come if they hear about the party?

4 If they don't help, their parents *will be* / *are* angry.

5 If you think carefully, I'm sure you *find* / *'ll find* a nice present for her.

6 There won't be many people at the match if the weather *gets* / *will get* worse.

7 If you *won't* / *don't* keep in touch with your friends, they'll lose interest in you.

8 ★★☆ Match the sentence halves.

0 I'll take the train | `d`
1 Will they come for lunch
2 If you don't tell Tracy about the situation,
3 I won't phone you
4 If they don't want to come to your party,
5 She'll only buy the phone
6 If people hear how much the tickets are,
7 Unless the teacher gives us really difficult homework,

a I'll finish it before 7 o'clock.
b you'll have to accept their decision.
c a lot of them won't go.
d unless Dad offers to drive me.
e if it isn't too expensive.
f how will she know?
g unless I change my plans.
h if we invite them?

9 ★★☆ Complete the text. Use the correct form of the verbs in the list.

be | not pass | invite | be | go | not let | miss

Dear Diary,
Not a great day today. Had a test in French. Unless I'm totally wrong, the results ⁰ **won't be** very good. If I ¹_____, I don't know what I'll do. My parents ²_____ me go to the cinema with Bryan tomorrow unless I pass. If I tell Bryan I can't go to the cinema with him, he ³_____ someone else. If he ⁴_____ with someone else, I ⁵_____ a film I'd love to see. But what if I wait and tell my parents later? Well, who knows how they'll react? I think that unless I come up with a brilliant idea, I ⁶_____ in trouble whatever I do. Well, one thing's for sure: next time I'll prepare better for my French test.

10 ★★★ Write first conditional questions. Then match them with the answers.

0 rain / what / you do
If it rains, what will you do? | `d`
1 watch TV tonight / what / you / watch
_____
2 what / you / buy / get / birthday money
_____
3 feel hungry / at break / what / you / eat
_____
4 what / you / do / not pass / the exam
_____
5 what / you / do / lose / your phone
_____

a I'll ask my mum for a new one.
b That won't happen!
c Nothing. I think I'll save the money.
d I'll stay at home.
e I'll watch a film.
f A sandwich or some biscuits.

11 ★★★ Answer four of the questions in Exercise 10 about you.

GET IT RIGHT! 👁
First conditional tenses

Learners sometimes use *will* instead of the present tense in the first conditional.

✓ I will be pleased if they *like* it.
✗ I will be pleased if they *will like* it.

Correct the following sentences.

0 I'll let you know if we'll be late.
I'll let you know if we're late.
1 If we have some help, there isn't a problem.
_____
2 I will wear a coat if it will be cold.
_____
3 They'll understand if you'll explain it.
_____
4 Will he go if the meeting will be at 7.00?
_____
5 If it won't rain, they'll have a picnic.
_____

Pronunciation
/f/, /v/ and /b/ consonant sounds
Go to page 119. 🔊

VOCABULARY

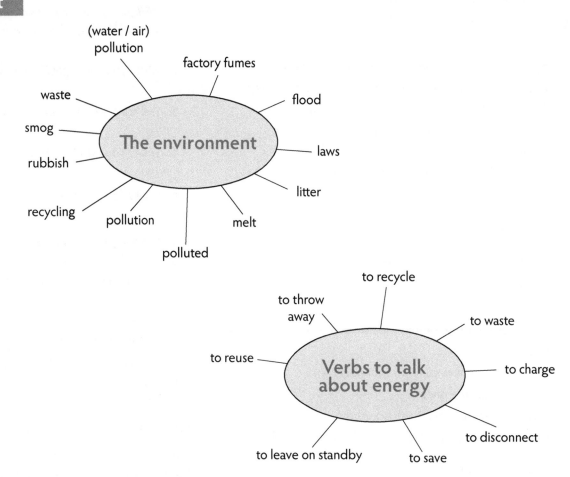

Key words in context

climate change	Experts say **climate change** is responsible for some of the hurricanes.
consequence	If I don't pass this test, the **consequences** will be serious. Dad won't take me to Disneyland!
damage	The fire did a lot of **damage** to the house.
deforestation	**Deforestation** is destroying large areas of tropical rainforest.
endangered species	We have to protect **endangered species** such as the black rhino.
energy	All the **energy** we need to heat the pool comes from the sun.
fear	Scientists **fear** the problems will become bigger over the next few years.
financial	**Financial** interests play a big role in deforestation.
fragile	Be careful how you hold it. It's **fragile** and breaks very easily.
generation	We have to think of the next **generation** and stop pollution.
global warming	Most people agree that **global warming** is making our Earth hotter and is causing problems with our weather.
industry	The financial **industry** in the UK makes more money than the manufacturing industry these days.
landscape	I saw a film about New Mexico and I was fascinated by the **landscape**.
ocean	Is the Atlantic **Ocean** bigger than the Pacific?
organism	The Great Barrier Reef is the only living **organism** you can see from space.
overfishing	Many kinds of fish are disappearing because of **overfishing**.
responsibility	Well, you're the boss, so it's your **responsibility**.
threat	Global warming is a **threat** to our future.
tiny	It's **tiny**. I don't think I've ever seen a bird so small.
tribe	The Amazon rainforest is home to more than 300 **tribes**.

The environment SB p.58

1 ★☆☆ **Write the words under the pictures.**

factory fumes | rubbish | flood | litter
pollution | waste | recycling | smog

1 *factory fumes*

2 _____

3 _____ , _____ , _____ ,

2 ★★☆ **Match the sentence halves.**

0 Many people think we need stricter   `g`

1 Plastic bags produce   ☐

2 If global warming continues, many glaciers ☐

3 Some parts of the world don't get enough rain, ☐

4 In many of the world's largest cities,   ☐

5 Recycling paper means   ☐

6 This river's water is very clean – it doesn't seem ☐

7 To help the environment, we should recycle   ☐

a while others get flooded all the time.

b will melt and this will be terrible.

c polluted at all.

d rubbish and we must never produce litter.

e far too much waste.

f smog and factory fumes cause bad air pollution.

g laws to protect the environment.

h we don't need to cut down so many trees.

Verbs to talk about energy SB p.61

3 ★★☆ **Circle the correct option: A, B, C or D.**

0 If you reuse something,
   A you throw it away.
   B you use it for the last time.
   C you waste a lot of energy.
   (D) you use it again.

1 Recycling helps to
   A understand pollution.
   B save energy.
   C throw things away.
   D waste energy.

2 It's better to disconnect electrical appliances
   from their
   A owners.   B smog.
   C power source.   D standby.

3 Certain whales belong to the world's
   A endangered tribes.
   B fragile organisms.
   C endangered species.
   D tiniest organisms.

4 Cutting down too many forests causes
   A deforestation.   B consequences.
   C responsibilities. D financial interests.

5 Experts say that a lot of damage has been done
   to the world's
   A energy.   B fear.
   C pollution.   D oceans.

6 The future of the world is everybody's
   A generation.   B damage.
   C trouble.   D responsibility.

7 Climate change is making the environment
   A tiny.   B fragile.
   C polluted.   D endangered.

4 ★★★ **Answer the questions.**

1 What do you think is the biggest threat to our
   environment and why?

   _____

   _____

2 How do you feel when you see someone throw
   litter on the street?

   _____

   _____

3 Have you ever told somebody not to pollute the
   environment? How did they react?

   _____

   _____

4 What positive examples do you know of people
   caring for the environment?

   _____

READING

1 REMEMBER AND CHECK **Answer the questions. Then check your answers in the article on page 57 of the Student's Book.**

0 What animals do people kill because they think they have special powers?
The black rhino.

1 Why are rare species of fish more in danger from overfishing than others?

_____

2 How much of the world is covered in forests?

_____

3 Why are people cutting down forests? (two reasons)

_____

4 How long have we already had the problem of rising sea water temperatures?

_____

5 What effects might it have on coastal cities if temperatures rise further?

_____

2 **Read the article quickly. Answer the questions.**

1 Who is the girl in the photo?

_____

2 Where is she from?

_____

3 Where did she give a speech?

_____

3 **Read the article again. Mark the sentences T (true) or F (false). Correct the false information.**

0 Severn was 12 when she managed to speak to the UN Assembly in Brazil. ☐ *T*

1 She got the money for the trip to Brazil from some friends at the United Nations. ☐

2 She spoke about a number of serious problems the world was facing. ☐

3 One topic she didn't talk about was the situation of human beings. ☐

4 When she finished, people stood up and clapped. ☐

5 The example of Severn shows that unless you're an adult, you can't make a difference to the world. ☐

4 **Imagine you have the chance to speak to the world leaders. What are you going to speak about and why? Write a short text (50–100 words).**

I am going to speak about ...

A young girl who made people listen and made a difference

Let's say that you're 12 years old, you feel strongly about something and you want to talk about it. Perhaps, though, you think that no one wants to hear what you have to say. Well, there are examples of young people who have made the adult world pay attention.

One example is Severn Cullis-Suzuki from Canada. Many years ago, when she was very young, she learned that the United Nations Assembly was going to meet in Brazil in 1992. Severn decided that she wanted not only to go there but also to say something. She started to raise money for the trip and when she was 12, she had enough for the 11,000-kilometre journey.

Severn was sure that she had something to say, and when she made her five-minute speech to the UN Assembly, she tried very hard to make an impact. Severn stood up and talked to the Assembly about a lot of things. She talked about environmental issues like pollution and the hunting of animals to extinction, but she also talked about the situation of children in many parts of the world, poor and starving children in particular. She contrasted them with children in richer countries who have more than they need and throw things away. Severn didn't pretend to have any answers, but her questions were a challenge to the world's leaders – questions about why the adults who run the world don't take more care of it and of the people who live in it.

Many people who heard her speech were crying at the end, and the audience gave her a standing ovation when she finished.

So, the lesson is that your age isn't the important thing. Severn showed that young people can make a difference, providing they're brave enough to believe in themselves. Who knows? Perhaps you could be another Severn.

DEVELOPING WRITING

An article to raise awareness about an environmental issue

1 **Read the extracts. Which of them ...**

1 outline a problem? [A] and [ ]

2 describe what will happen if nothing is done? [ ] and [ ]

3 suggest what to do? [ ] and [ ]

A These attractive birds live near rivers. They eat frogs and other small animals. The species is endangered because the birds cannot find enough food any more. Cities are getting bigger and bigger, and humans destroy their natural habitat.

B If we don't stop pollution, the temperature will rise further. If the Earth gets hotter, it will have dramatic consequences. If we don't act now, it might be too late.

C First, we must introduce new laws to stop deforestation. The laws should say that big companies that have earned millions from producing paper have to invest some of their money to save the rainforest.

D Some people believe that having a wild animal in a cage at home is something special. This is why, every year, thousands of exotic animals die on their way to other countries and continents.

E First, we need to make sure that there are enough trains and buses so that people can travel to work on public transport. Then we need to let people know what will happen if everybody uses their car all the time.

F We need to do something now. If the level of the oceans keeps rising, many small islands will be flooded. People and animals will die. This will all happen for sure unless we all change things now.

2 **Complete the sentences from Exercise 1 with linking words.**

0 The species is endangered _because_ they cannot find enough food any more.

1 Some people believe that having a wild animal in a cage at home is something special. _____, every year, thousands of exotic animals die on their way to other countries and continents.

2 This will all happen for sure _____ we all change things now.

3 We need to make sure that there are enough trains and buses _____ that people can travel to work.

4 We need to let people know what will happen _____ everybody uses their car all the time.

● If you want to raise awareness about an environmental issue, you need to structure your text very carefully.

3 **Read the phrases in the list. Which ones are ...**

1 a description of a problem?
   Every year, we lose ... _____

2 talking about consequences?
   _____

3 a suggested action?
   _____

● If we don't stop now, there will be ...
● Unless people begin to change their behaviour, it might be too late.
● In five years' time, most of the animals will ...
● Then we have to ...
● Forty per cent of the species in that area are in danger.
● The air in big cities is terribly polluted.
● We must introduce new laws to stop ...
● Every year, we lose ...
● First we need to ...
● The species is endangered because ...
● We might have bigger problems soon.

4 **Write an article about an environmental issue (about 200 words). If you have already written about a global problem (page 63 of the Student's Book), write about a local problem now. If you have written about a local problem, write about a global issue.**

● Describe the problem.
● Explain what will or might happen if nothing changes.
● Make suggestions to solve it.

LISTENING

1 🔊 25 **Listen to the conversations and match them with the pictures.**

A ⬜

B ⬜

> Oh!
> Your birthday!
> Sorry, I forgot!

C ⬜

2 🔊 25 **Listen again and answer the questions.**

CONVERSATION 1

0 Where does Vicky's aunt live?
   She lives in the US.

1 What has she invited Vicky to do?
   _____

2 What does Vicky invite Henry to do?
   _____

CONVERSATION 2

3 What's Isaac planning to do at the weekend?
   _____

4 Who's he going to invite?
   _____

5 Why isn't Anne so happy about his plans?
   _____

CONVERSATION 3

6 What's Oliver going to do on Sunday?
   _____

7 Where's he going to do it?
   _____

DIALOGUE

1 🔊 25 **Match the sentences. Then listen again and check.**

0	She's invited me.	e
1	Are you all right?	⬜
2	Are you sure Mike and Nick are excited too?	⬜
3	I'll be able to see all the drivers up close.	⬜
4	Well, you don't think it's a great idea, do you?	⬜

a Yeah, I'm fantastic. I'm planning something great for the weekend.

b Wow! How come?

c Well, to be honest, no.

d I haven't told them. But I'm sure they'll think it's great.

e I know, and I think that's wonderful.

2 **Complete the phrases with the missing vowels.**

0 Wh*at* *a* gr*ea*t id*ea*!

1 Th __ t's __ m __ z __ ng!

2 Th __ t s __ __ nds __ xc __ t __ ng!

3 W __ w!

4 __ h, r __ __ lly?

5 H __ w __ xc __ t __ ng!

6 C __ __ l!

7 __ ncr __ d __ bl __ !

3 **Write two short conversations about people telling their friends some exciting news.**

◼◼◼ TRAIN TO THINK ◼◼◼

Recognising different text types

1 **Read the extracts and write the text types. Check your answers on page 60 of the Student's Book.**

0 Hi Jane, Gr8 you'll come over to my place on Sunday. Got some cool DVDs. Love, B
   Text message

1 Pop in and check out our vegetables – grown by local farmers and brought to you daily by us.
   _____

2 A spokesman for SpaceLive said to reporters on Tuesday that the company was thinking of sending plants to the moon.
   _____

3 He opened his eyes. He had no idea where he was, but he knew the place was dangerous.
   _____

4 Jane, please feed the cat. Food's in the fridge. See you tonight, Mum
   _____

5 Monday: another cool day at school. Science project interesting, working with Lisa. Tomorrow photography club.
   _____

Help with reading: skimming a text

- When you skim a text, you don't read it word for word. You read it quite quickly to try to understand the main idea.

- Skimming is a useful technique to decide if you want to read a text or not. By skimming a text, you'll get a general idea of what's in it, so you can decide if it makes sense for you to read it in detail. Many people use skimming when they read a newspaper – they only want to read a story in detail if it's something they're interested in, and to decide that, they skim the text first.

Tip: skimming a text

- To skim a longer text, read the title, the first two paragraphs, one or two paragraphs in the middle and the last paragraph (or the last two).
- To skim a shorter text, read the beginning, a little bit from the middle and the ending.
- To skim a paragraph, read the first and the last sentences.
- To skim, move your eyes faster than you would normally do, and don't read every word.
- Photos and other visuals (for example, graphs) may help you to get the main idea of a text too.

1 Skim the paragraph and write what the main idea is. Use the tip to help you.

For most people, watching mega sports events such as the Olympic Games is an enjoyable activity. Millions of people sit in front of their TVs every four years, and countries are very keen to become the hosts of the Games. However, all this fun has consequences for the environment, and they aren't fun at all. Mountains of litter are produced at big sporting events, from plastic bottles to plates, from packaging to food waste and tons of paper. An enormous amount of resources is needed to build the stadiums and the places where athletes, officials and journalists live during the event. And all those thousands of people need to travel from far away. It's no secret that this causes air pollution.

This text is about:

_____

2 Skim the longer text and write what the main idea is. Use the tip to help you.

London Zoo is one of Britain's top attractions and is the world's oldest scientific zoo, founded over 180 years ago. It can be found in the heart of London, in Regent's Park. It is run by the Zoological Society of London.

Although this zoo is located in the middle of the city, it still has plenty of animals to see, including lions, camels, giraffes, penguins, tigers, monkeys and meerkats. In fact, there are 750 different species, making it one of the largest collections of animals in the UK.

The zoo is divided up into many different areas, which are great fun to explore and help make it one of London's most popular tourist attractions.

Gorilla Kingdom
Gorilla Kingdom is home to a colony of Western Lowland gorillas, which live together with other primates.

The African Bird Safari
The African bird house is full of beautiful birds that share the environment with other animals from Africa.

Butterfly Paradise
As visitors walk through this area, they are surrounded by free-flying butterflies from Africa, South-East Asia and Central and South America, seeking out plants on which to feed and rest.

Lions and tigers
London Zoo is home to a family of Asian lions and a pair of Sumatran tigers, and visitors can get very close to the zoo's beautiful but endangered big cats.

Aquarium
The Aquarium is split into three areas and features many exotic and weird fish and a stunning coral reef.

Penguin Beach
Opened in 2011, Penguin Beach is England's biggest penguin pool. It has underwater windows to allow visitors to watch the birds swimming.

There are several places where you can buy food and drink, and souvenirs can be purchased in the gift shop.

London Zoo is located at the north end of Regent's Park, a ten-minute walk through the park from Regent's Park tube station on the Bakerloo line, or a shorter walk from Camden Town tube station on the Northern Line.

This text is about:

_____

CONSOLIDATION

LISTENING

1 ◀))26 **Listen to the conversation. Tick (✓) A, B or C.**

1 Who chose the name of the band?

   A Alice ☐

   B Ian ☐

   C Ben ☐

2 What instrument does Ian play in the band?

   A keyboard ☐

   B guitar ☐

   C drums ☐

3 What instrument does Liz play?

   A trumpet ☐

   B saxophone ☐

   C violin ☐

2 ◀))26 **Listen again. Answer the questions.**

0 Why is the band called The Green Warriors?

   To show that they care about the environment.

1 What does Ben do in the band?

   _____

2 What do Jessica and Lucy play in the band?

   _____

3 How long has Liz been playing the saxophone?

   _____

4 Where does the band practise?

   _____

GRAMMAR

3 (Circle) **the correct words.**

I've ⁰*worked /* *been working* at the local nature reserve for three months. I spend half my time at the reserve and half my time visiting schools. I've ¹*already visited / been visiting* about 20 schools in the local area. I think it's very important to talk to teenagers. If they ²*don't / won't* learn how to love the environment, there ³*isn't / won't be* much future for our world. One of the projects I've ⁴*worked / been working* on for the last few months is trying to stop the building of a new power station. Unless we ⁵*do / don't do* something to stop it, it ⁶*will / won't* cause serious problems for the local wildlife because they want to build it on an important nesting site for many rare birds. I've ⁷*already written / been writing* about 30 letters to the local politician, but so far he hasn't ⁸*replied / been replying* to me.

4 **Complete the sentences with the correct present perfect simple or continuous form of the verbs in brackets.**

0 Jane Cooper ___*has been*___ (be) a famous writer for a long time.

1 She _____ (write) over thirty novels now.

2 She _____ (write) novels for many years.

3 She _____ (make) a lot of money.

4 Thousands of people _____ (send) her letters.

5 She _____ (reply) to all of them!

6 Since last month, she _____ (think) about her next novel.

7 But she still _____ (not decide) what the new novel will be about.

VOCABULARY

5 **Match the sentence halves.**

0 Marty James started writing ___*g*___

1 He started ☐

2 They played their first ☐

3 The band entered ☐

4 And they won ☐

5 For their prize they got the chance ☐

6 The song was ☐

7 It soon entered ☐

8 Next month the band are going ☐

a a talent show.

b to record a single.

c downloaded over 200,000 times.

d on a national tour.

e gig in the school hall.

f the competition.

g songs when he was 12.

h a band a year later.

i the pop charts.

6 **Complete the words.**

Three simple ways to make a difference.

● ⁰S *ave* your plastic bags and ¹r_____ them next time you go shopping – don't ²t_____ them ³a_____.

● ⁴R_____ your rubbish – sort out the plastic from the paper and the glass.

● ⁵D_____ electronics at night. Don't leave them on ⁶s_____. It just ⁷w_____ power.

DIALOGUE

7 Complete the conversation with the phrases in the list. There is one phrase that you don't need.

~~What a great idea.~~ | So what's the matter?
I can't wait. | No way. | If you say so
There's no point in | How exciting!
I'm just a bit upset. | What's up, Jennie?

JENNIE   Have you heard the news?

ROB   What news?

JENNIE   We're having a school concert to raise money for the Clean Up Our Air campaign.

ROB   0 *What a great idea.*

JENNIE   And our band's playing.

ROB   1 _____

JENNIE   Isn't it? 2 _____

[Two days later]

ROB   3 _____. You don't look very happy.

JENNIE   It's nothing. 4 _____

ROB   5 _____

JENNIE   Remember the school concert I told you about the other day? Well, it's been cancelled.

ROB   6 _____

JENNIE   Yes, it's true. The headmaster decided it wasn't a good idea.

ROB   It's not right. We've got to do something. I'm going to talk to him now.

JENNIE   7 _____ trying to change his mind. It's not happening!

READING

8 Read the article. Mark the sentences T (true) or F (false).

0 'This Is My Dream' was Kashy's first song. `F`

1 Five years after he wrote 'This Is My Dream', Kashy decided to put it online. ☐

2 A Hong Kong TV station wanted to use this song to advertise their shows. ☐

3 Kashy contacted the TV station and asked to perform in Hong Kong. ☐

4 People in Hong Kong thought Kashy was famous in his home country. ☐

5 Kashy is now starting to be successful as a musician. ☐

Kashy Keegan always wanted to be a pop star and spent years trying to make it happen. In 2007, when he was 22, he wrote what he felt would finally be his big hit, a song called 'This Is My Dream', but it never happened. As the years passed, he started to give up on his musical career and found other jobs. In 2012, he decided to upload the song to a music sharing website called Reverbnation. He hoped someone might hear it and like it.

A few months later, he received an email from Universal Music in Hong Kong. They were starting a new TV station and they wanted to use 'This Is My Dream' as the theme tune to one of their shows. Kashy was really excited and made a deal for $5,000 to allow the TV station to use his song.

The TV station invited Kashy to come over to Hong Kong and perform. He accepted the invitations and was met by hundreds of fans. Everyone there thought he was a big star in the UK. He had to try and explain that back home, no one knew who he was. A little later, Kashy was playing the song live on stage to more than 30,000 screaming fans. After the show, he gave lots of interviews and signed hundreds of autographs. The next day, he saw his face in all the local newspapers and the song went to number one in the iTunes charts.

Two days later, Kashy was back in his job in London, but he is flying out to Hong Kong again soon to play his first live shows. His pop dream is finally happening.

WRITING

9 Write a short text (about 120–150 words) about your favourite song. Include this information:

- who the song is by
- when it was first released
- how popular it became
- what the song is about
- why you like it

PRONUNCIATION

UNIT 1
Sentence stress

1 Complete the sentences with the correct words from the list. Circle the stressed word in each sentence.

~~brilliant idea~~ | a joke | to be famous one
changed forever | dangerous places | definitely do
fantastic time | is for living | had a terrible
help you | never heard | the new café

0 That's a ___*brilliant idea*___ !

1 Can I _____ ?

2 Then one day, her life _____ .

3 I know. Let's go to _____ !

4 We should _____ it!

5 We had a _____ .

6 She travels to some of the most _____ to take photos.

7 They're going _____ day.

8 Then my aunt _____ car accident.

9 I've _____ him complain.

10 'Life _____ ,' she said.

2 ◀))06 Listen, check and repeat.

UNIT 2
Word stress

1 Write the verbs from the list in the correct columns.

~~concentrate~~ | believe | forget | guess | know
think | recognise | remember | suppose

1	One syllable	2	Two syllables	3	Three syllables
	_____		_____		*concentrate*
	_____		_____		_____

2 ◀))07 Listen, check and repeat.

3 Which syllable is stressed? Write the verbs in the correct columns.

~~believe~~ | concentrate | consider | discuss
explain | imagine | listen | motivate
recognise | remember | study | wonder

Oo	oO	Ooo	oOo
_____	*believe*	_____	_____
_____	_____	_____	_____

4 ◀))08 Listen, check and repeat.

UNIT 3
Words ending with schwa /ə/

1 Complete the sentences with comparative forms of the adjectives in the list.

~~tidy~~ | early | funny | good
old | slow | tall | quiet

0 My sister's a lot ___*tidier*___ than me. Her bedroom is always clean.

1 There's too much noise here – let's go somewhere _____ .

2 He's very clever and much _____ at Maths than me.

3 Mum has to go to work at 8 o'clock; she gets up _____ than the rest of us.

4 My brother's 1.72 metres. He's _____ than me.

5 Jake's fourteen and his sister's ten. He's _____ than her.

6 You're driving too fast. Could you please go a little _____ ?

7 This comedy show is much _____ than the one we saw last week.

2 ◀))11 Listen, check and repeat.

3 Write the comparatives from Exercise 1 in the correct columns. <u>Underline</u> the stressed syllable. Remember that the final syllable 'er' is never stressed. It has the schwa /ə/ sound.

Two syllables	Three syllables
better	*earlier*

4 🔊12 **Listen again, check and repeat.**

UNIT 4
The short /ʌ/ vowel sound

1 Circle the word in each line that doesn't have the /ʌ/ sound (e.g. the sound in *son*, *one* and *done*).

```
0   a son      b one      c done     d (dog)
1   a fun      b won      c home     d come
2   a shout    b young    c much     d tongue
3   a enough   b cousin   c you      d love
4   a must     b mother   c nose     d doesn't
5   a trouble  b jump     c other    d note
6   a love     b stuff    c funny    d ground
7   a put      b wonder   c under    d nothing
8   a could    b some     c lovely   d brother
9   a Sunday   b Monday   c over     d cover
10  a none     b use      c monkey   d another
11  a good     b blood    c touch    d couple
```

2 🔊16 **Listen, check and repeat.**

UNIT 5
Strong and weak forms of *been* /biːn/ and /bɪn/

1 Match the statements (1–6) with the responses (a–g).

0 Have you <u>been</u> to London? __e__

1 Where have you been? You're covered in dirt! ____

2 You look ill. ____

3 You need to go to the director's office, now. ____

4 Look at your face. It's so red! Where have you been? ____

5 How long has it been since you saw John? ____

6 The girls are tired. ____

a I know. I've been to the doctor's

b I've been working in the garden.

c It's been a long time – more than three months.

d They've been playing football.

e Yes, I have. I've been going there every summer since I was ten.

f I've been at the beach all day. I forgot my sun cream.

g I've already been.

2 🔊19 **Listen, check and repeat.**

3 Circle the strong forms of *been* /biːn/ and underline the weak forms of *been* /bɪn/.

4 🔊19 **Listen again, check and repeat.**

UNIT 6
/f/, /v/ and /b/ consonant sounds

1 🔊23 **Listen and circle the word you hear.**

```
0  a (few)  b view     3  a ferry  b very
1  a fast   b vast     4  a leaf   b leave
2  a fan    b van      5  a off    b of
```

2 🔊23 **Listen, check and repeat.**

3 Circle the correct words to complete the sentences.

0 They went out in Bill's dad's (boat) / *vote*.

1 That's a *berry* / *very* good idea.

2 She wants to be a *vet* / *bet* when she's older.

3 I wore my *best* / *vest* clothes to the party.

4 He drives a white *van* / *ban* for his job.

4 🔊24 **Listen again, check and repeat.**

GRAMMAR REFERENCE

UNIT 1
Present perfect with *just, already* and *yet*

We often use the present perfect with the words *just / already / yet*.

1. We use *just* before the past participle to say that something happened a short time ago.

   *They've **just** come back from their holiday.*

2. We use *already* at the end of a sentence or before the past participle to show surprise, or to emphasise that something has been done, or finished, sooner than expected.

   *Have you finished **already**?*
   *No food thanks – I've **already** eaten.*

3. We use *yet* at the end of negative sentences and questions, to emphasise that something hasn't happened but probably will in the future.

   *Have you finished your homework **yet**?*
   *I haven't played that game **yet** (but I will).*

Present perfect vs. past simple

1. We use the past simple to talk about events which are complete and finished, or 'before now', at the time of speaking.

   *I **saw** you in town yesterday. Who **were** you with?*

2. We use the present perfect to connect the past and 'now' (at the time of speaking).

   *I **haven't seen** you this week. Where **have you been**?*

UNIT 2
Present perfect with *for* and *since*

1. We can use the present perfect to talk about something that began in the past and continues to be true in the present.

   *We've **lived** here for ten years (= and we still live here.)*

2. We talk about the time between when something started and now with *for* or *since*.

   - We use the word *for* when we mention a period of time from the past until now.
     for half an hour / for three months / for ages
   - We use the word *since* when we mention a point in time in the past.
     since six o'clock / since 2012 / since last weekend

a, an, the or no article

1. We use *a, an* before a singular, countable noun to talk about something for the first time in a conversation.

   *Look – there's **a horse** in the garden!*
   *Do you want **an apple**?*
   We also use *a / an* when we are not talking about a specific thing.
   *I haven't got **a** computer.*

2. We use *the* before a noun when it is clear which thing(s) or person/people we are talking about.

   ***The** apples in our garden are delicious.*
   *Have you got **the** book? (= the book we were talking about before)*
   ***The** woman next door is really friendly.*
   We also use the when there is only one thing that exists.
   *Look at **the** moon!*

3. We use no article (zero article) before plural countable nouns, and before uncountable nouns, when we are talking about things in general.

   ***Cars** are expensive.*
   ***Love** is the most important thing.*

UNIT 3
Comparative and superlative adjectives (review)

1. When we want to compare two things, or two groups of things, we use a comparative form + *than*.

   *My sister is **older than** me.*
   *My old phone was **more expensive than** my new one.*
   *The film is **better than** the book.*

2 With short adjectives, we normally add *-er*. With longer adjectives (more than two syllables), we normally don't change the adjective – we put *more* in front of it.

hot → hotter   short → shorter   clever → clever**er**
interesting → **more** interesting
exciting → **more** exciting

3 Some adjectives are irregular – they have a different comparative form.

good → better   bad → worse   far → further

(not) as … as

When we want to say that two things are the same (or not the same) we can use *(not) as* + adjective + *as*.

She's **as tall as** her mother now.
This question is**n't as easy as** the last one.

Making a comparison stronger or weaker

We can make a comparison stronger or weaker by using *much / far*, *a lot* or *a little / a bit*. These words come before the comparison.

His computer is **far better** than mine.
His bike was **much more expensive** than mine.
He lives **a little further** from school than I do.

Adverbs and comparative adverbs

1 We use adverbs to describe verbs — they say how an action is or was performed.

She <u>shouted</u> **angrily**. <u>Run</u> **quickly**!
They <u>got</u> to the theatre **early**.
We can also use adverbs before adjectives.
It was **really** <u>cold</u> on Sunday.
The coffee was **incredibly** <u>hot</u>, so I couldn't drink it.

2 Most adverbs are formed by adjective + *-ly*.

slow → slow**ly**   nice → nice**ly**
If the adjective ends in *-le*, we drop the *-e* and add *-y*.
incredible → incredib**ly**   possible → possib**ly**
If the adjective ends in consonant + *-y* we change the *-y* to *-i* and add *-ly*.
angry → angr**ily**   lucky → luck**ily**
hungry → hungr**ily**

3 Some adverbs are irregular – they don't have an *-ly* ending.

good → well   fast → fast   hard → hard
early → early   late → late

4 To compare adverbs, we use the same rules as we do when we compare adjectives. With short adverbs, we add *-er* or *-r*, and *than* after the adverb.

I worked **hard**, but Sue worked **harder than** me!

5 With longer adverbs, we use *more* (+ adverb) + *than*.

She does things **more easily than** me.

6 To compare the adverb *well*, we use *better … than*. To compare the adverb *far*, we use *further … than*.

He cooks **better than** me.
London to Mumbai is **further than** London to New York.

UNIT 4
Indefinite pronouns

1 We can use the words *every / some / no / any* together with *one / thing / where* to make compound nouns.

everyone = all the people
everything = all the things
everywhere = all the places
someone = a person, but we don't know who
something = a thing, but we don't know which
somewhere = a place, but we don't know where
no one = none of the people
nothing = none of the things
nowhere = none of the places
anyone = any person / any of the people
anything = any of the things
anywhere = any of the places

2 These words are all singular.

Something smells nice. **No one's** here. **Nothing was** found. **Everywhere was** full. **Someone has** opened my desk.

3 We don't use negatives with *nothing* and *no one*. We use *anything* or *anyone* instead.

I do**n't** know **anyone** here.
(NOT I ~~don't know no one~~ here.)

all (some / none / any) of them

With other nouns and pronouns, we use *all of / some of / none of* + plural or uncountable noun/pronoun.

All of them are yours.   **Some of** the teachers are really nice.
None of my friends called me yesterday.
Do **any of** you know the answer?

should(n't), had better, ought to

1 *Should*, *had ('d) better* and *ought to* are all used to give advice.

2 *Should* and *ought to* both mean '*I think it's (not) a good idea for you/me/him (etc.) to do this*'.

You **should do** more exercise. (= I think it is a good idea for you to do more exercise.)
She **shouldn't talk** in class. (= I think it is not a good idea for her to talk in class.)
We **ought to** leave now. (= I think it is a good idea for us to leave now.)

3 The meaning of *had better* is often stronger. The speaker wants to say that there are negative consequences if the person ignores the advice.

*I'd **better run**.* (or I'll be late)
*You**'d better not talk** in class.* (or the teacher will be angry)

4 *Should, had better* and *ought to* are all followed by the infinitive of another verb.

*You **should be** more careful.   I **ought to eat** more fruit.   We**'d better hurry** or we'll be late.*

5 *Should* and *had better* form the negative by adding *not* afterwards.

*They **shouldn't be** so rude.*
*We**'d better not** stay out late.*

> We make *ought to* negative by putting *not* after *ought* (but we don't use this form very often).

*You **ought not to** make so much noise.*

UNIT 5
Present perfect continuous

1 The present perfect continuous is formed with the present tense of *have* + *been* + the *-ing* form of the verb.

*I've **been reading** since breakfast.*
*Have you **been sitting** here all day?*

2 Sentences with the present perfect always connect the present and the past. We often use the present perfect continuous to talk about activities which started in the past and are still continuing now.

*She's **been running** for an hour.* (= She started running an hour ago, and she is still running.)

3 We also use the present perfect continuous to talk about actions with a result in the present. These actions may or may not be complete.

*I'm tired because I've **been working**.*
*Jack's feeling ill because he **hasn't been eating** well.*

4 We also use the present perfect continuous to talk about actions which began in the past and continue to the present, but perhaps we are not doing the action at the time of speaking.

*We've **been studying** Spanish for six months.*
(= We started studying six months ago, and we are still studying, but we're not studying at this exact moment.)

Present perfect simple vs. present perfect continuous

1 We use the present perfect simple to show that an action is finished, or to focus on what (and how much) we have completed in a period of time.

*I've **written** an email.*
*I've **written** twelve emails this morning.*

2 We use the present perfect continuous to show that an action is still going on, or to focus on how long something has been in progress.

*I've **been reading** this book for two days.*
*I've **been reading** detective stories for years.*

> **Compare the sentences:**
> *She's **been writing** books for many years.*
> *She's **written** over twenty books.*

UNIT 6
will (not), may (not), might (not) for prediction

1 We can use the modal verb *will* (*'ll*) or *will not* (*won't*) to make predictions about the future.

*Don't worry about the exam – it **won't be** difficult.*

2 We use *might/might not* or *may/may not* to make less certain predictions about the future.

*It **might rain** this afternoon – if it does, then I **may not** go the match.*

First conditional / unless in first conditional sentences

1 We use the first conditional to talk about possible actions / situations in the future, and their (possible) results.

If I finish my homework, I'll go out.

2 We often make conditional sentences by using *if* + subject + present simple in the *if* clause, and *will/won't / might/might not* in the main clause.

*If I **have** time this afternoon, I'**ll go** for a walk.*
*We **might go** out tonight if there'**s** nothing good on TV.*

3 We can also use the word *unless* in conditional sentences – it means *if not*.

*She **won't come unless** you **ask** her.* (= She won't come if you don't ask her.)

4 There are two clauses in these sentences. We can put the main clause first, or the *if/unless* clause first. When the *if/unless* clause comes first, there is *a comma (,) after it.*

***Unless** you tell me, I won't know what to do.*
*I won't know what to do **unless** you tell me.*

IRREGULAR VERBS

Base form	Past simple	Past participle
be	was / were	been
beat	beat	beaten
become	became	become
begin	began	begun
break	broke	broken
bring	brought	brought
build	built	built
buy	bought	bought
can	could	–
catch	caught	caught
choose	chose	chosen
come	came	come
cost	cost	cost
cut	cut	cut
do	did	done
draw	drew	drawn
drink	drank	drunk
drive	drove	driven
eat	ate	eaten
fall	fell	fallen
feel	felt	felt
fight	fought	fought
find	found	found
fly	flew	flown
forget	forgot	forgotten
get	got	got
give	gave	given
go	went	gone
grow	grew	grown
hang	hung	hung
have	had	had
hear	heard	heard
hit	hit	hit
hurt	hurt	hurt
hold	held	held
keep	kept	kept
know	knew	known
lead	led	led
leave	left	left
lend	lent	lent

Base form	Past simple	Past participle
let	let	let
lie	lay	lain
light	lit	lit
lose	lost	lost
make	made	made
mean	meant	meant
meet	met	met
pay	paid	paid
put	put	put
read / riːd/	read /red/	read /red/
ride	rode	ridden
ring	rang	rung
rise	rose	risen
run	ran	run
say	said	said
see	saw	seen
sell	sold	sold
send	sent	sent
set	set	set
shoot	shot	shot
show	showed	shown
sing	sang	sung
sit	sat	sat
sleep	slept	slept
speak	spoke	spoken
spend	spent	spent
stand	stood	stood
steal	stole	stolen
strike	struck	struck
swim	swam	swum
take	took	taken
teach	taught	taught
tell	told	told
think	thought	thought
throw	threw	thrown
understand	understood	understood
wake	woke	woken
wear	wore	worn
win	won	won
write	wrote	written

Acknowledgements

The authors and publishers acknowledge the following sources of copyright material and are grateful for the permissions granted. While every effort has been made, it has not always been possible to identify the sources of all the material used, or to trace all copyright holders. If any omissions are brought to our notice, we will be happy to include the appropriate acknowledgements on reprinting.

The Zoological Society of London for the text on p. 61 from the London Zoo website. Reproduced with permission;

The Guardian for the text on p. 63 adapted from 'Experience: I became a pop star overnight. The next morning I found out my song had gone to number one, beating Lady Gaga, Justin Bieber and Katy Perry' by Kashy Keegan, *The Guardian*, 15/03/2014. Copyright ©Guardian News & Media Ltd 2014;

Corpus

Development of this publication has made use of the Cambridge English Corpus (CEC). The CEC is a computer database of contemporary spoken and written English, which currently stands at over one billion words. It includes British English, American English and other varieties of English. It also includes the Cambridge Learner Corpus, developed in collaboration with Cambridge English Language Assessment. Cambridge University Press has built up the CEC to provide evidence about language use that helps to produce better language teaching materials.

English Profile

This product is informed by the English Vocabulary Profile, built as part of English Profile, a collaborative programme designed to enhance the learning, teaching and assessment of English worldwide. Its main funding partners are Cambridge University Press and Cambridge English Language Assessment and its aim is to create a 'profile' for English linked to the Common European Framework of Reference for Languages (CEF). English Profile outcomes, such as the English Vocabulary Profile, will provide detailed information about the language that learners can be expected to demonstrate at each CEF level, offering a clear benchmark for learners' proficiency. For more information, please visit www.englishprofile.org

Cambridge Dictionaries

Cambridge dictionaries are the world's most widely used dictionaries for
learners of English. The dictionaries are available in print and online at dictionary.cambridge.org. Copyright © Cambridge University Press, reproduced with permission.

The publishers are grateful to the following for permission to reproduce copyright photographs and material:

T = Top, B = Below, L = Left, R = Right, C = Centre, B/G = Background

p. 5: ©sumnersgraphicsinc/iStock/360/Getty Images; p. 14 (T): ©George C. Beresford /Hulton Archive/Getty Images; p. 14 (B): ©Pictorial Parade /Archive Photos/Getty Images; p. 16: ©BEI/Gregory Pace/REX; p. 19: ©bikeriderlondon/Shutterstock; p. 20: ©Lightspring/ Shutterstock; p. 21 (0): ©Krasimira Nevenova/Shutterstock; p. 21 (1): ©Björn Höglund/Alamy; p. 21 (2): ©moodboard/360/Getty Images; p. 21 (3): ©Elnur/Shutterstock; p. 21 (4): ©belchonock/iStock/360/ Getty Images; p. 21 (5): ©Paul Fleet/iStock/360/Getty Images; p. 21 (6): ©MOT-Foto/iStock/360/Getty Images; p. 21 (7): ©greenleaf123/ iStock/360/Getty Images; p. 22: ©Ashwin Kharidehal Abhirama/ iStock/360/Getty Images; p.22 (B/G): ©blue67design/Shutterstock; p. 24 (TL): ©DWaschnig/Shutterstock; p. 24 (TR): ©Karkas/Shutterstock; p. 24 (BL): ©Ron Ellis/Shutterstock; p. 24 (BR): ©ACE STOCK LIMITED/Alamy; p. 33: ©Siri Stafford/Digital Vision; p. 34 (TL): ©trappy76/iStock/360/ Getty Images; p. 34 (TR dvd and box): ©Henry Leib/iStock/360/Getty Images; p. 34 (TR dancer): ©R. Gino Santa Maria/Shutterstock; p. 34 (BL): ©GeorgeMPhotography/Shutterstock; p. 34 (BR): ©Minerva Studio/iStock/360/Getty Images; p. 45: ©INTERFOTO/Alamy; p. 48 (TL): ©Stockbyte/Getty Images; p. 48 (TCL): ©Balefire/Shutterstock; p. 48 (TCR): ©serji_o/iStock/360/Getty Images; p. 48 (TR): ©Stockbyte/ Getty Images; p. 48 (BL): ©VvoeVale/iStock/360/Getty Images; p. 48 (BCL): ©Hemera Technologies/PhotoObjects.net/360/Getty Images; p. 48 (BCR): ©Hemera Technologies/PhotoObjects.net/360/Getty Images; p. 48 (BR): ©Stockbyte/Getty Images; p. 50: ©AGF s.r.l./REX; p. 51: ©MediaPunch/REX; p. 53: ©Kalenik Hanna/Shutterstock; p. 57 (T): ©rustyl3599/iStock/360/Getty Images; p. 57 (C): ©SlobodanMiljevic/ iStock/360/Getty Images; p. 57 (B): ©Justin Kase zfivez / Alamy; p. 58: ©*/Kyodo/Newscom; p. 61: ©Dan Kitwood /Getty Images Sport/Getty Images; p. 63: ©M & Y News Ltd/REX

Cover photographs by: (TL): ©Tim Gainey/Alamy; (C): ©hugh sturrock/ Alamy; (R): ©Andrea Haase/iStock/Getty Images Plus, Getty Images; (BL): ©Oliver Burston/Alamy.

The publishers are grateful to the following illustrators:
David Semple 5, 8, 15, 34, 40, 46, 60, 66, 73, 75, 80, 90, 108;
Julian Mosedale 4, 10, 29, 37, 42, 54, 64, 72, 74, 78, 86, 95, 114

The publishers are grateful to the following contributors:
Blooberry: text design and layouts; Claire Parson: cover design; Hilary Fletcher: picture research; Leon Chambers: audio recordings; Karen Elliott: Pronunciation sections; Matt Norton: Get it right! exercises